The Beast of Hungary

Juan de la Cuesta Hispanic Monographs

SERIES: UCLA Center for 17th- and 18th-Century Studies:
The *Comedia* in Translation and Performance, N.º 18

FOUNDING EDITOR
Tom Lathrop †
University of Delaware

PUBLISHER
Michael P. Bolan
University of Delaware

EDITOR
Michael J. McGrath
Georgia Southern University

EDITORIAL BOARD
Vincent Barletta
Stanford University

Annette Grant Cash
Georgia State University

David Castillo
State University of New York-Buffalo

Gwen Kirkpatrick
Georgetown University

Mark P. Del Mastro
College of Charleston

Juan F. Egea
University of Wisconsin-Madison

Sara L. Lehman
Fordham University

Mariselle Meléndez
University of Illinois at Urbana-Champaign

Eyda Merediz
University of Maryland

Dayle Seidenspinner-Núñez
University of Notre Dame

Elzbieta Sklodowska
Washington University in St. Louis

Noël Valis
Yale University

Félix Lope de Vega y Carpio

The Beast of Hungary

Translated by

The UCLA Working Group
on the *Comedia* in Translation and Performance:

David Chibukhchian   Diana Echeverria Palencia
Barbara Fuchs   Marta Albalá Pelegrín
Isaac Giménez   Victoria Rasbridge
Brenda Saraí Jaramillo   Cristian Reyes
Rachel Kaufman   Rhonda Sharrah
Robin Kello   Rebecca Ogden Smith
Javier Patiño Loira   Madeline Werner
Aina Soley Mateu   Jesslyn Whittell
Laura Muñoz

Juan de la Cuesta
Newark, Delaware

Our translations are free to use for educational and performance purposes with attribution to Diversifying the Classics, under a Creative Commons Attribution 4.0 International License. We are happy to discuss and consult on performances and adaptations. Notify us at diversifyingtheclassics.ucla@gmail.com prior to use.

Copyright © 2025 by Barbara Fuchs. All rights reserved.

Juan de la Cuesta Hispanic Monographs
An imprint of LinguaText, LLC
103 Walker Way
Newark, Delaware 19711 USA
(302) 453-8695

www.JuandelaCuesta.com

MANUFACTURED IN THE UNITED STATES OF AMERICA
ISBN: 978-1-58871-412-1

Table of Contents

The *Comedia* in Context 7
A Note on the Playwright... 11

Introduction
    Victoria Jane Rasbridge and Brenda Saraí Jaramillo 13
Pronunciation Guide...25

The Beast of Hungary
    Characters 26
    Act I..27
    Act II 66
    Act III 110

The *Comedia* in Context

THE "GOLDEN AGE" OF Spain offers one of the most vibrant theatrical repertoires ever produced. At the same time that England saw the flourishing of Shakespeare on the Elizabethan stage, Spain produced prodigious talents such as Lope de Vega, Tirso de Molina, and Calderón de la Barca. Although those names may not resonate with the force of the Bard in the Anglophone world, the hundreds of entertaining, complex plays they wrote, and the stage tradition they helped develop, deserve to be better known.

The *Diversifying the Cla*ssics project at UCLA brings these plays to the public by offering English versions of Hispanic classical theater. Our translations are designed to make this rich tradition accessible to students, teachers, and theater professionals. This brief introduction to the *comedia* in its context suggests what we might discover and create when we begin to look beyond Shakespeare.

COMEDIA AT A GLANCE

The Spanish *comedia* developed in the late sixteenth and early seventeenth centuries. As Madrid grew into a sophisticated imperial capital, the theater provided a space to perform the customs, concerns, desires, and anxieties of its citizens. Though the form was influenced by the Italian troupes that brought *commedia dell'arte* to Spain in the sixteenth century, the expansive corpus of the Spanish *comedia* includes not only comic plays, but also histories, tragedies, and tragicomedies. The varied dramatic template of the *comedia* is as diverse as the contemporary social sphere it reflects.

While the plays offer a range of dramatic scenarios and theatrical effects, they share structural and linguistic similarities. Roughly three thousand lines, they are usually divided into three different *jornadas*, or acts. Plots move quickly across time and space, without much regard for the Aristotelian unities of action, time, and place. The plays are written in verse, and employ different forms for different characters and situations: a lover may deliver an ornate sonnet in honor of the beloved, while a servant offers a shaggy-dog story in rhymed couplets. The plays' language is designed for the ear rather than the eye, with the objective of pleasing an audience.

The *comedia* was performed in rectangular courtyard spaces known as *corrales*. Built between houses of two or three stories, the *corral* offered seating based on social position, including space for the nobles in the balconies, women in the *cazuela*, or stewpot, and *mosqueteros*, or groundlings, on patio benches. This cross-section of society enjoyed a truly popular art, which reflected onstage their varied social positions. A *comedia* performance would have included the play as well as songs, dances, and *entremeses*, or short comic interludes, before, after, and between the acts. As the first real commercial theater, the corral was the place where a diverse urban society found its dramatic entertainment.

What's at Stake on the *Comedia* Stage?

Comedias offer a range of possibilities for the twenty-first century reader, actor, and audience. The plays often envision the social ambitions and conflicts of the rapidly-growing cities where they were performed, allowing a community to simultaneously witness and create a collective culture. In many *comedias*, the anonymity and wealth that the city affords allow the clever to transcend their social position, while wit, rather than force, frequently carries the day, creating an urban theater that itself performs urbanity. An important subset of *comedias* deal with topics from national history, exploring violence, state power, the role of the nobility, and religious and racial difference.

The *comedia* often examines social hierarchies that may be less rigid than they first appear. Whether the dominant mode of the play is comic, tragic, historical, or a mixture, its dramatic progression often depends on a balancing act of order and liberty, authority and transgression, stasis and transformation. The title of Lope de Vega's recently rediscovered *Women and Servants*, in which two sisters scheme to marry the servant-men they love rather than the noblemen who woo them, makes explicit its concerns with gender and class and provides a view of what is at stake in many of the plays. Individuals disadvantaged by class or gender often challenge the social hierarchy and patriarchy by way of their own cleverness. The *gracioso* (comic sidekick), the *barba* (older male blocking figure), and the lovers appear repeatedly in these plays, and yet are often much more than stock types. At their most remarkable, they reflect larger cultural possibilities. The *comedia* stages the conflicting demands of desire and reputation, dramatizing the tension between our identities as they are and as we wish them to be.

Among the many forms of passion and aspiration present in the *comedia*, female desire and agency are central. In contrast to its English counterpart, the Spanish stage permitted actresses to play female roles, thus giving playwrights the opportunity to develop a variety of characters for them. While actresses became famous, the powerful roles they played onstage often portrayed the force of female desire. In Lope's *The Widow of Valencia*, for example, the beautiful young widow Leonarda brings a masked lover into her home so as not to reveal her identity and risk her reputation or independence.

The presence of actresses, however, did not diminish the appeal of the cross-dressing plot. One of Tirso's most famous plays, *Don Gil of the Green Breeches*, features Doña Juana assuming a false identity and dressing as a man in order to foil the plans of her former lover, who is also in disguise. Dizzying deceptions and the performance of identity are both dramatic techniques and thematic concerns in these plays. Gender, like class, becomes part of the structure the *comedia* examines and dismantles, offering a powerful reflection on how we come to be who we are.

Remaking Plays in Our Time

In Lope's witty manifesto, the *New Art of Making Plays in Our Time*, he advises playwrights to stick to what works onstage, including plots of honor and love, strong subplots, and—whenever possible—cross-dressing. For Lope, the delight of the audience drives the process of composition, and there is little sense in a craft that does not entertain the public. Lope's contemporaries followed this formula, developing dramas that simultaneously explore the dynamics of their society and produce spectacle. For this reason, early modern Hispanic drama remains an engaging, suspenseful, often comic—and new—art to audiences even four hundred years later.

The *Diversifying the Classics* project at UCLA, engaged in translation, adaptation, and outreach to promote the *comedia* tradition, aims to bring the entertaining spirit of Lope and his contemporaries to our work. Rather than strictly adhering to the verse forms of the plays, we seek to render the power of their language in a modern idiom; rather than limiting the drama as a historical or cultural artifact, we hope to bring out what remains vibrant for our contemporary society. Given that these vital texts merit a place onstage, we have sought to facilitate production by carefully noting entrances, exits, and asides, and by adding locations for scenes whenever possible. Although we have translated every line, we assume directors will cut as appropriate for their own productions. We hope that actors, directors, and readers will translate our work further into new productions, bringing both the social inquiry and theatrical delight of the *comedia* to future generations of audiences.

A Note on the Playwright

FÉLIX LOPE DE VEGA Y CARPIO (1562–1635) is the towering figure of the *comedia*. Born in Madrid to parents who had migrated to the capital from Spain's northern regions, he saw in his youth the emergence of the *corral* theaters where he would go on to make his name. In his *New Art of Making Plays in Our Time*, Lope formalized the conventions of the *comedia*, outlining the elements of the vibrant new art of which he was the master. He composed hundreds of plays, in addition to poetry and prose, earning him the name *Fénix de los ingenios* ("Phoenix of Wits"), as the expression *es de Lope* ("it's by Lope") became a shorthand for praising quality.

In his own time, Lope's fame arose out of his prodigious literary talent as well as his colorful biography, for the playwright's erotic life often left him on the wrong side of the law. After being rejected by the actress Elena Osorio in the 1580's, Lope penned a series of satirical poems attacking her family, and was exiled from Madrid for the offense. Though Lope would go on to take orders in 1614, love affairs that defied early modern Spanish religious and legal codes continued to dominate his life and he left an unknown number of illegitimate children.

Despite these scandals and his eventual position as secretary to the Duke of Sessa, Lope was a truly successful commercial playwright, who earned income as well as fame through his literary efforts. Today he is best remembered for the drama he came to define—the quick, witty *comedia*. After Calderón's *Life Is a Dream*, Lope's *Fuenteovejuna* is the best-known *comedia* in the English-speaking world, and others such as *Peribañez* and *The Dog in the Manger* exemplify the well-constructed Lopean plot. Miguel de Cervantes, his contemporary, may not have meant it as a compliment when he called Lope a "monster of nature" (*monstruo de la naturaleza*), as the two masters were not on friendly terms. Yet Lope's prodigious output was fundamental to defining the theater of the age that spanned his life. The monster of nature left us many gifts.

Introduction
Victoria Jane Rasbridge
and Brenda Saraí Jaramillo

Lope de Vega's *The Beast of Hungary* (*El animal de Hungría*, 1617) takes the audience on a wild journey, from the forests of Hungary to the courts of kings. With humor and pathos, the play explores eternal questions about justice, loyalty, and what makes us "human"—in all our frailty and nobility. The extremes of the human heart are on display, from murderous jealousy to the first buddings of young love, making us question what truly separates man from beast.

The Plot

Act I starts with Teodosia, the former queen of Hungary, encountering Lauro, a low-ranking nobleman living in the countryside. She is disguised as a beast, and Lauro identifies her as the creature that has been terrorizing and stealing from his village. Teodosia tells him her story: she is the daughter of the king of England, married to Primislao, king of Hungary. When she first arrived in Hungary, Teodosia was lonely and sent for her sister, Faustina, to keep her company. But Faustina fell in love with Primislao and secretly determined to steal Teodosia's throne. She claimed Teodosia was having an affair with the prince of Scotland and plotting with him to murder Primislao. Primislao believed Faustina, and sent his men to kill Teodosia. Taking pity on the innocent queen, the soldiers left her alive in the woods, though they reported to Primislao that she was dead. Primislao then married Faustina, who became the new queen. Lauro, sympathetic, promises to not tell anyone what Teodosia has revealed to him and to visit her in the cave where she lives in hiding.

Nearby, the town officials hold a meeting to discuss important affairs. Pascual, a villager, interrupts by announcing that the king of Hungary will go hunting in the nearby woods. They all hope he can hunt down the beast.

Faustina and Primislao arrive with their entourage. She is noticeably pregnant. The townspeople greet the monarchs and tell them about the beast. Faustina begins to feel ill with the heat and sun; Primislao suggests a nap in the woods and leaves her behind as he proceeds with the hunt. Alone, she goes into labor. Teodosia encounters Llorente, a villager, in the woods. He tells her that the king and his wife have come. Faustina emerges from the woods with her newborn baby. Vowing revenge, Teodosia jumps out and startles Faustina, who does not recognize the beast as her sister. As Faustina faints from fright, Teodosia takes the baby and disappears. When Primislao and his entourage return, Faustina comes to and explains what happened. Primislao calls a massive hunt for the beast.

Meanwhile, three Spanish noblemen come ashore. They are following orders from the count of Barcelona to abandon the young Felipe, his illegitimate grandson, in the wilds of Hungary. Felipe's mother is the count's daughter; his father is the son of the king of Naples, and the count's nephew. Displeased at their secret marriage, the count has ordered his men to get rid of the child. Despite the young boy's tender pleas, they abandon him in Hungary. Lauro and Llorente then discover Felipe. Lauro, who can speak Spanish, hears his sad tale, then promises to take him in and raise him as his own son.

Twenty years pass between Act I and the opening of Act II. Teodosia is arguing with Rosaura, the child she took from Faustina so many years ago and raised as her own daughter. Rosaura likes to go off into the woods by herself, which Teodosia has forbidden for fear she will encounter villagers on the hunt. Rosaura is frustrated with Teodosia's many rules, and wants to know who her father is. Teodosia tells her that she, Teodosia, is Rosaura's mother and father. Faced with Rosaura's disbelief, Teodosia tries again and tells her that the sun is her father. Rosaura then reveals that she has seen a man for the first time, naked and bathing in the river. She concludes that she must have seen the sun, her father. She innocently asks her mother if the sun has burned her, because she is aflame with passion. Teodosia is mortified. She attempts to convince her daughter that men are dangerous. Meanwhile, Belardo, a villager, tells Lauro and Felipe that he saw not one, but two beasts in the woods. Lauro knows that the older beast is Teodosia, but doesn't know who the younger beast could be. Once alone, Lauro and Felipe talk about Felipe's secret noble background. Lauro makes Felipe promise that he will one day return to Spain to claim his throne and assume his identity as the count of Barcelona's rightful heir. Reluctantly, Felipe agrees.

Rosaura is wandering in the woods when she encounters Felipe again, now alone. She makes the sign of the cross to scare him off, but the two identify each other as Christians. As they converse, they quickly fall for each other. When Felipe leaves, Rosaura becomes jealous of Silvana, a villager who has also wandered into the woods. Thinking Felipe might love Silvana instead, Rosaura attacks her. Teodosia arrives and stops Rosaura, but is dismayed to find out that Rosaura is in love. Felipe returns, and the two lovers commit to each other. Soon the villagers appear, hunting Rosaura because Silvana has informed them of her attack. Felipe attempts to stop the villagers and in the ensuing scuffle he kills one of them. The villagers take him prisoner, while Rosaura vows to rescue him. Lauro begins to tell them of Felipe's secret noble heritage in order to save him, but Felipe makes him stop. The mob decides to take Felipe to King Primislao to be punished. As she attempts to save Felipe, Rosaura is apprehended and chained. Rosaura and Felipe pledge their undying love for each other.

In Act III, Primislao and Faustina discuss their two captives. An ambassador from Barcelona arrives. He announces that Felipe's grandfather has passed away, and his parents, now the rightful countess and count of Barcelona, seek their long lost son, Felipe. Primislao agrees to help find him. Teodosia enters, disguised as a peasant. Faustina asks what she knows of the beast they have captured. Teodosia tells them that since the day of Queen Teodosia's death, the village has been terrorized by a beast. Teodosia implies that the death was under suspicious circumstances, which frustrates Primislao, who still believes her death was righteous, and frightens Faustina, who is afflicted with a guilty conscience. Teodosia, disguised, goes on to report that ever since the attack on Faustina and her baby's subsequent disappearance twenty years ago, the village has recorded sightings of two beasts, one older than the other. Suspicious, Faustina asks Teodosia to find out if the dead baby Faustina was presented with twenty years ago was actually hers, or if her baby survives somewhere. Primislao also asks the disguised Teodosia to act as the captive beast's keeper. Rosaura is brought to the room, and Teodosia signals she must pretend not to know her. The admiral of Hungary enters. He announces that the king of England, father to both Teodosia and Faustina, plans to attack Hungary, for he now knows that Teodosia's apparent death was a plot and wants revenge. He is aided by the prince of Scotland, who is outraged that he was named as Teodosia's supposed lover. As Primislao prepares for war, a magistrate enters to request the execution order for Felipe. Rosaura argues that she should be put to death instead. Primislao orders her to be executed, too. Rosaura, fighting with her captors, pledges to free Felipe.

Later, Teodosia observes, unseen, a meeting between Faustina and the admiral. Faustina reveals that the admiral supported her plot to kill her sister.

She now plans to poison Primislao so he will never discover her murderous plot against Teodosia. She promises to marry the admiral and make him king if he defends her against her approaching father. Teodosia hears everything. Primislao, Lauro, and the ambassador of Barcelona enter. Lauro tells them that Felipe is the grandson of the count of Barcelona and asks that he be freed from prison and pardoned for his crime. Felipe tells Rosaura that she will be his queen. When Felipe is released, Rosaura asks to sit at the king's table and dine with him, but instead she is tied to a pillar. The king of England, the prince of Scotland, and soldiers enter and confront Primislao. Teodosia reveals that Rosaura is Faustina's baby, and that she is actually the former queen, long believed dead. Primislao immediately embraces his long-lost wife, agrees to marry Rosaura to Felipe, and pardons Faustina for her crimes.

Queenship in the Play

In early modern Spain, queens were at the center of familial and political systems of power and instrumental to the efficient running of the monarchy. They were wives, sisters, daughters, and mothers whose royal lineage and marital alliances brought them global influence. Although queens have historically been seen as secondary figures, inferior to their male counterparts, they often held positions of power in their own right. Female monarchs often stepped into the role of regent when a king or prince was absent, at war, visiting other parts of their kingdom, or simply too young to rule. In fact, due to what Merry E. Wiesner-Hanks calls a series of "dynastic accidents" in Europe, an unprecedented number of women occupied the highest positions of power throughout the early modern period (28).

A female monarch could play a number of different roles: queen consort, queen regent, dowager queen, or even queen regnant. What is more, she could play different roles throughout her lifetime. While each role demanded its own skill set, all were undermined by a fundamental paradox: as a ruler, the queen was expected to act with authority and enjoy absolute power over her people, but as a woman, she was considered innately inferior to half of her kingdom.

Queens were, therefore, often the subject of intense social and political scrutiny, and their power was repeatedly called into question. This was particularly true during the period in which *The Beast of Hungary* was written. At this time, Margaret of Austria, queen consort to King Philip III of Spain, was the subject of a long and vicious smear campaign led by the duke of Lerma, the king's favorite (*privado*). Like countless men before him, Lerma used scandal and slander to challenge Margaret's alleged power over the king. Accusing her of disloyalty to Spain, Lerma tried to hem her in at court and even to separate the royal couple by sending the king on countless travels, hoping this physical distance would inspire an emotional one.

The duke of Lerma's accusation—that Margaret of Austria was not acting in the interest of the Spanish people, but that of her kingdom of birth—preys on the fact that royal women were often geographically transplanted. Following marriage, a queen was expected to leave her homeland and familiar court to take up residence in the kingdom of her new husband. With this move came the expectation that she would embrace her husband's culture and partake in his kingdom's traditions. Yet, as an ambassador for her own family and kingdom, she was also expected to remain loyal to her heritage and publicly display her close connection to it. The queen was paradoxically valued because of her familial connections, heritage, and difference, but also expected to forget her loyalties and assimilate into a new society.

While a queen's ability to navigate these paradoxes influenced her perceived success as a ruler, it was her ability to produce a legitimate, preferably male, heir that ultimately determined her success—hence Faustina's anxiety at not being able to produce an heir in this play. Fulfilling the role of royal mother was of such great importance that many early modern queens spent the majority of their married lives pregnant, and death in childbirth was the leading cause of queenly mortality. Many queens "were literally bred to death" (Beem, 4).

Maternity

The overlapping prerogatives of queenship and motherhood are crucial to Lope's play. Being a mother was fundamental to being queen, and the central conflict of the plot is the struggle over who can be the best queen-and-mother. *The Beast of Hungary* actually hinges on the battle between two female sovereigns—Teodosia and Faustina—whose attempts to secure power rely on their proximity to, and influence over, legitimate heirs.

Teodosia and Faustina embody the various vices and virtues associated with the figure of the maternal sovereign. Faustina is ambitious and cunning enough to assume a higher birthright and become queen, despite her status as a second daughter. Furthermore, her relative youth, with its corresponding associations of health and fertility, soon leads to pregnancy, making her a powerful contender to the throne. However, Faustina's ambition and efficacy are also indicators of her cruelty, and her inability to mother any of her children, due to miscarriages, stillbirths, and kidnapping, implies divine punishment for her malicious plotting. Like Lady Macbeth, who offers up her maternity in exchange for being "unsexed" enough to carry out masculine-coded violence, Faustina can never be a mother following the success of her political schemes. In this play, the lack of a child is punishment for an unacceptable performance of female sovereignty.

Unlike Faustina, Teodosia does not biologically produce a child, but instead exercises social mothering as an adoptive parent. As Act II begins, it becomes clear that Teodosia has instructed Rosaura in logic and reasoning, and has relied on religious doctrine to guide her moral conscience. In this way, she is responsible for Rosaura's moral instruction and intellectual development, which corresponds to the definition of the word *educación* in Spanish. This emphasis on evaluating a maternal sovereign's success via the *educación* of her heirs perhaps explains why the child born at the end of Act I has no distinguishing features—ungendered and unnamed, it is the perfect empty slate to receive the teachings of its queen-and-mother. The two decade gap between Act I and Act II, in which Rosaura grows into a young woman, covers a generation, the time "within which values, wealth, goods, and morals are passed through family ties from one generation to the next" (Halberstam, 5). This use of time grounds the present moment of the play within the historical past of the royal family while simultaneously pointing towards a more just future for Hungary. In the play, this time is entirely controlled by Teodosia, who assumes responsibility for the royal succession as she raises the first living child born to the king and his new queen. Teodosia's morality in the political sphere—shown in her decision not to hurt Faustina in Act I and later pardon her in Act III—implies an ethics that makes her a commendable maternal figure to Rosaura, the future queen of Hungary. In Teodosia's approach to Rosaura, Lope suggests a good queen needs to not simply produce heirs, but to instruct them properly. As (adoptive) mother to the future of the kingdom, she is performing her duty as queen *in absentia*. Thus the play's ultimate sympathetic maternal sovereign is not the woman best suited for politics or even childbearing, but the one best suited for moral mothering.

Virginity, Sexuality, and Carnal Knowledge

Ironically for a play about mothering, virginity is a key measure of successful female sovereignty. Teodosia recalls the immediate solitude and culture shock she experienced upon moving to Hungary from England, which her husband rectified by taking a long absence from the castle to fetch her sister, Faustina, to keep Teodosia company. Teodosia's lack of access to the king, due initially to his long absence and subsequently to her sister's infatuation, implies that her marriage was never close. Teodosia's physical, and presumably emotional, distance from her husband then becomes the target of Faustina's malicious plotting: she accuses the rightful queen of engaging in infidelity and sexual promiscuity with the prince of Scotland. The supposed affair is carried out discursively via letters that Faustina forges as evidence. Teodosia is socially excoriated and politically excised from the monarchy. It is important to note, however, that Faustina's accusations imply planned promiscuity and infidelity at both a geographic and temporal distance. In other words, Teodosia's purported crime is *plotting* political and sexual treason, not actually committing it in the present time and place of the play. In this way, Teodosia's implied moral purity is preserved, despite the accusations levied against her.

The emphasis on virginity as a condition of female success is challenged most directly by Rosaura, who rebels against her mother's insistence on abstinence. Beyond functioning as comic relief, Rosaura's intense interest in human sexuality stands in stark contrast to both Teodosia and Faustina. Teodosia, on the one hand, needs Rosaura to perform a virginity legible to the royal court in order to confirm her own chastity by proxy. Though Rosaura is not yet sexually active, her frank curiosity regarding sexual activity undermines Teodosia's hope for redemption. On the other end of the political and sexual spectrum is Faustina, whose weapon of choice is her own sexuality. With it, she can express her uncurbed ambition and secure alliances in her favor: first with the king of Hungary to dethrone her sister the queen, then with the admiral of Hungary to kill her husband and wage war against her father, the king of England. This political maneuvering via female sexuality is something that is wholly absent in Rosaura. Her earnest interest challenges the binary distinction between virginity and monstrosity as represented by Teodosia and Faustina. Instead, Rosaura manages to unite Faustina's politicized sexuality with Teodosia's virginal innocence, thereby constructing a unique womanhood that embraces carnal knowledge for its own sake. Rosaura reminds us that this instinctual thirst for knowledge, intellectual or carnal, need not be constrained by inherited gender norms: "Mother, don't be angry at my desire to know" (1118-9).

Early Modern Monsters

Rosaura is vividly marked by her relentless "desire to know" (1119), to understand what it means to be a human. As she attempts to figure this out, Rosaura draws on her upbringing as a beast, intertwining Renaissance understandings of the anatomical, moral and intellectual capacities of monsters, animals, and humans.

During the period, people believed that the animal body and the human body were almost identical, differentiated only by humans' possession of an inorganic, rational soul. It was humans' immaterial soul that allowed them to look up to heaven, and bestowed them with common sense, fantasy, imagination, thought, and memory. It was also the rational soul that housed humans' emotions, passions, and appetites, allowing them to love, desire, hope, fear, and despair. Standing in stark contrast to humanity is the monster—anything abnormal or outside the natural order. In the Renaissance, a monster was most typically identified by a "monstrous" birth—that is, the birth of a child with any physical deformities. But a monster could also be anything extraordinary, anything made imperfect or different by either excess or deficiency. Because a monster was primarily distinguished by its difference (good or bad), its characterization shows what a society deemed unacceptable or undesirable.

The distinction between animals, humans, and monsters is constantly called into question in Lope's play, as the audience is asked to weigh who, or what, is a real monster when presented with Teodosia, Rosaura, and Faustina. The most obvious embodiment of the monster, or beast, is Teodosia, the former queen consort of Hungary and princess of England who transforms herself into a wild beast in order to survive in the mountains where she has been abandoned. Teodosia's transformation involves using an array of costumes, disguises, and a veil of savagery. Yet her savagery is largely reported rather than acted out on stage. The villagers tell many stories of her thefts and supposed attacks, but when she actually appears on stage, her character does not match her disguise: she speaks to Lauro with honesty in Act I; she stops Rosaura from attacking Silvana in Act II; and she forbids Faustina's execution in Act III. Despite her external appearance as a monster, it is clear that Teodosia possesses a rational soul and is of a gentle disposition.

Rosaura, by contrast, is raised by Teodosia in the belief that she is an animal. Although the audience does not see her grow up, thanks to the two decade gap between Act I and Act II, the stories of the villagers and Rosaura's own remarks make it clear that she was raised physically, if not morally, to live as a wild animal. Over the course of the play, however, it becomes apparent that Rosaura is unlike the other animals with whom she shares her home. Constantly asking questions and using logic to solve the mysteries for which she is denied answers, Rosaura attempts to learn how she came to exist. This culminates in the middle of Act III when Rosaura, having come to the palace to rescue Felipe, is bound by chains and tied to a pillar. Standing alone on the stage, she asks herself:

> Oh soul hidden beneath this rough exterior,
> are you capable of feeling?
> Then my soul says: "Can you not see that I am?"
> And of understanding?
> "In understanding I am naturally blessed."
> And of acting with free will?
> "Do you not see it in the one I choose to love,
>   despite the suffering it brings?"
> And what of memory?
> "That too, and at any moment,
> I am ready to fly on its wings."
> Well then, my soul,
> if you love, understand, and remember,
> and your love is led by your understanding and memory,
> then do not lose your mind,
> but hold onto those faculties that God has given you
> to distinguish good from bad,
> punishment from glory. (2909-26)

Rosaura here outlines the faculties that differentiate a human from an animal: feeling, understanding, memory, and acting with free will. Her quest for knowledge and sound reasoning clearly demonstrate her rationality, a concept alien to both beasts and monsters. As Rosaura blossoms sexually in the play, so too does she blossom intellectually; her transformation encourages the audience to look beyond appearances or first perceptions, to question representation and find the reality that lies beneath.

Faustina, on the other hand, is presented as unequivocally human. Her schemes to usurp her sister's throne and her seduction of the admiral of Hungary to maintain her position as queen demonstrate her ability to think and act rationally. At no point does she physically adopt the dress of a beast, nor does she leave the confines of the palace and court in the play, except to give birth in Act I. Yet it is Faustina who acts with the greatest savagery. Over the course of play, she commits numerous atrocities: falsely accusing Teodosia of infidelity with the prince of Scotland; sanctioning her sister's unjust punishment and murder; and seducing the admiral of Hungary to get him to help kill her husband, King Primislao. If we revisit Rosaura's definition of what it is to be a human—to feel, understand, love and use "those faculties that God has given you to distinguish good from bad, punishment from glory"—we might doubt Faustina's humanity altogether. While she evidently acts with plentiful free will, her actions appear devoid of feeling, understanding, or love, as she crosses the line between good and evil. Her repeated sanction of murder in pursuit of power hints at the fact that she may, in fact, be the most monstrous of all. Through the careful construction and juxtaposition of these three female characters, *The Beast of Hungary* invites the audience to reflect upon what truly makes a monster, and ultimately ask themselves who *The Beast of Hungary* may truly be.

About This Translation

This translation is a collaborative effort of UCLA's *Comedia* in Translation Working Group, based on an edition of the play prepared by the Biblioteca Virtual Miguel de Cervantes. We have also consulted Christopher John Follett Michell's 2006 thesis, titled *Lope de Vega,* El Animal de Hungría: *Estudio crítico y traducción al inglés*. Our perennial goal is to make the translated text attractive for contemporary directors and performers. To that end, we have chosen to translate into prose. In addition to facilitating performance, translating into prose foregrounds the play's cheeky emphasis on teenage rebellion, budding sexuality, and first love, which we hope will resonate with contemporary audiences of all ages.

Production History

First published in 1617 in Lope's *Parte IX*, *The Beast of Hungary* was probably written around 1608-1612. No original manuscript exists to give us insight into the play's early performance history, and modern editions unfortunately offer no clues regarding historical performance. Recent productions include La Poltrona at the University of California Davis (2015), and the Madrid theater group Colectivo Állatok, who toured their production across Spain in 2021 and presented it at the LA Escena Festival of Hispanic Classical Theater at UCLA in 2022. Red Bull Theater (New York) presented the first reading of our translation in September 2024 (see below).

References and Further Reading

C. Beem. *Queenship in Early Modern Europe.* Red Globe Press, 2020.

C.J. Follett Michell. *Lope de Vega,* El animal de Hungría: *estudio crítico y traducción al inglés*. UNAM, 2006.

J. Halberstam. *In a Queer Time and Place: Transgender Bodies, Subcultural Lives.* NYU Press, 2005.

S.G. Morley and C. Bruerton. *The Chronology of Lope de Vega's Comedias: With a Discussion of Doubtful Attributions, Based on a Study of his Strophic Versification.* MLA, 1940.

Lope de Vega. *El animal de Hungría*. Biblioteca Virtual Miguel de Cervantes, 2000. http://www.cervantesvirtual.com/obra/el-animal-de-hungria--0/

———. *Arte nuevo de hacer comedias en este tiempo*. Biblioteca Virtual Miguel de Cervantes, 2003. https://www.cervantesvirtual.com/obra/arte-nuevo-de-hacer-comedias-en-este-tiempo--0/

M. Wiesner-Hanks. "Women's Authority in the State and Household in Early Modern Europe," in *Women Who Ruled: Queens, Goddesses, Amazons in Renaissance and Baroque Art*, ed. Annette Dixon. Merrell, 2002.

Our translation of *The Beast of Hungary* was given an early staged reading by Red Bull Theater in September 2024, as part of our ongoing Hispanic Golden Age Classics collaborative series (http://www.redbulltheater.com/the-beast-of-hungary).

Red Bull Theater Cast

Rosaura: Isabel Arraiza
Faustina: Shirine Babb
Llorente/Riselo/Lidio/King of England: Jimonn Cole
Felipe/Pascual: Darryl Gene Daughtry Jr.
Bartolo/Arfindo/Belardo/Ambassador: Jill Durson
Barber/Fulgencio/Velardo/Servant/Warden/Pablos: Zachary Fine
Benito/Silvana/Fenicio/Magistrate/Notary/Servant: Ismenia Mendes
Teodosia: Maria-Christina Oliveras
Town Crier/Huntsman/Magistrate/Servant/Admiral: Sean Runnette
Primislao: Matthew Saldivar
Selvagio/Plácido/Tirso/Celio/Squire: Han Van Sciver
Lauro: Chauncy Thomas

Red Bull Production Team

Director: Nadia Guevara
Stage Manager: Jenn McNeil
Assistant Stage Manager: Jessica Fornear
Video Services: Merelis Productions
Associate Producer: Joana Tsuhlares
Producing Director: Nathan Winkelstein
General Manager: Sherri Kotimsky

Pronunciation Guide

Each vowel in Spanish has just one sound. They are pronounced as follows:

    a - AH   e - EH   i - EE   o - OH   u - OO

The <u>un</u>derlined <u>syl</u>lable in each word is the <u>accent</u>ed one.

Teodosia: TEH-OH-<u>DOH</u>-SEE-AH
Rosaura: ROH-<u>SOW</u>-RAH (ow as in "ouch")
Faustina: FOW-<u>STEE</u>-NAH (ow as in "ouch")
Primislao: <u>PREE</u>-MEES-LAH-OH
Felipe: FEH-<u>LEE</u>-PEH
Lauro: <u>LOW</u>-ROH (ow as in "ouch")
Fulgencio: FOOL-<u>HEN</u>-SEE-OH
Arfindo: AHR-<u>FEEN</u>-DOH
Plácido: <u>PLAH</u>-SEE-DOH
Selvagio: SEHL-<u>VAH</u>-HEE-OH
Bartolo: <u>BAHR</u>-TOH-LOH
Benito: BEH-<u>NEE</u>-TOH
Llorente: YOH-<u>REHN</u>-TEH
Pascual: PAHS-<u>KWAHL</u>
Belardo: BEH-<u>LAHR</u>-DOH
Tirso: <u>TEER</u>-SOH
Riselo: REE-<u>SEH</u>-LOH
Gil: HEEL
Silvana: SEEL-<u>VAH</u>-NAH
Fenicio: FEH-<u>NEE</u>-SEE-OH
Lidio: <u>LEE</u>-DEE-OH
Celio: <u>SEH</u>-LEE-OH
Pablos: <u>PAH</u>-BLOHS
Fabio: <u>FAH</u>-BEE-OH

Characters

TEODOSIA, former queen of Hungary
FAUSTINA, current queen of Hungary
PRIMISLAO, king of Hungary
ROSAURA
FELIPE
LAURO
FULGENCIO, Spanish nobleman
ARFINDO, Spanish nobleman
PLÁCIDO, Spanish nobleman
SELVAGIO, town official
BARTOLO, town official
BENITO, villager
LLORENTE, villager
PASCUAL, villager
BELARDO, villager
TIRSO, villager
RISELO, villager
GIL, villager
SILVANA, villager
FENICIO, Hungarian nobleman
AMBASSADOR of Barcelona
LIDIO, page
CELIO, page
FABIO, page
PABLOS, jester
ADMIRAL of Hungary
King of ENGLAND
Prince of SCOTLAND
SQUIRE of the king of England
HUNTSMAN
BARBER
TOWN CRIER
MAGISTRATE
NOTARY
WARDEN
SERVANT

The Beast of Hungary

ACT I

SCENE 1

Enter TEODOSIA, *dressed in hides, and* LAURO *chasing her with a javelin*

TEODOSIA   Help me, nimble feet!
Save my wretched life
so that I may see this through.

LAURO   Stop, fearsome monster!

TEODOSIA   If I am so fearsome,
why aren't you afraid of me,
brave youth?

LAURO   My natural courage
is more powerful than fear.
Although my clothes are humble,   10
I am noble.

TEODOSIA   What are you after?

LAURO   To kill you or capture you.

TEODOSIA *reveals her face, pushing her hair to the side*

TEODOSIA Would you kill me *now*?

LAURO Oh my God!

TEODOSIA Have I surprised you?

LAURO Yes, with your rare beauty.
How could nature
in all its variety
fashion such a face   20
in this frigid wilderness?
For years, the peasants have fled from you.
But you should be loved, rather than feared,
and beguiled with the sweet lures of love.
Tell me about yourself,
if I may deserve such favor.
My eyes tell me you are a beautiful nymph,
or perhaps a mysterious sphinx.[1]
How could you have stolen
so much food and cattle   30
from the village?

TEODOSIA I get very hungry.

LAURO It made the peasants so afraid of you...

TEODOSIA And a good thing too!
Their fear has kept them away.

LAURO Such a heavenly face on the body of a beast!
If you had wings,

---

1 *Nymph*: A minor nature deity of Greek myth. *Sphinx*: Also a Greek mythological creature—with the head of a woman, the body of a lion, and the wings of an eagle—but, unlike the nymph, associated with female monstrosity.

	I'd take you for a harpy
	who would face a new Hercules.
	If you were at sea, 40
	I'd take you for a siren
	who enchants with her song.²

TEODOSIA   It was only a matter of time
            before my misfortune caught up to me.
            I know you won't leave me alone now,
            since you dared to chase me
            and look upon me.
            I see I will have to tell you my story.

LAURO   That's all I want.

TEODOSIA   Listen closely, young man. 50

LAURO   I won't be the only one.
            Everything around us,
            the birds and the wind,
            will be all ears.

TEODOSIA   I am Queen Teodosia,
            wife of Primislao,
            king of Hungary—
            though I wish I had never been.

LAURO   You are the queen, my lady?

TEODOSIA   For God's sake, young man, 60
            wait until I finish my story.
            The case is well-known,
            but I want you to hear it from me.

---

    2   *Harpy; siren; Hercules*: Mythological figures—respectively: half-woman, half-bird monster; alluring but deadly womanlike beings depicted in Homer's *Odyssey*; demigod and (male) hero who fought many monsters.

When I was newly wed and newly arrived
in Hungary from England,
I felt homesick in a foreign land.
I pleaded with my husband, the king,
to send for my younger sister, Faustina,
that she might comfort me.
This my father allowed.   70
My husband went to fetch her
but, on the way back,
she fell blindly in love with him,
and started to covet what was mine.
As soon as my sister set foot in Hungary,
I welcomed her with joyous celebrations.
All the while, she was plotting my demise.
Faustina was as unhappy to see me
as I was glad to see her.
She claimed she was sad   80
because she was far away from home.
She grew sick with envy and jealousy,
and the only thing that could cure her
was when my husband visited her.
One day, she told him
that I had loved the prince of Scotland in my youth,
and had never been happy in our marriage.
She also claimed that I had sent
a thousand letters to Scotland,
inviting the prince to come to my garden in secret.   90
Not only would I gladly let him in
if he brought his soldiers,
I would also serve them the head
of Primislao, my husband,
as they say that deceitful wife Scylla did in myth.[3]

---

3   *Scylla*: The reference is to a Greek princess who betrayed her father for love of his enemy King Minos of Crete, but the name also suggests the deadly female monster paired with Charybdis in the *Odyssey*. Notably, in the story Minos is disgus-

All this she claimed I had promised.
The king was easily deceived,
either because he was shown
a few counterfeit letters,
or simply because he loved her.   100
He ordered two of his trusted servants
to bring me to these mountains
and throw me to the wild beasts.
They left me here,
prey to gnashing teeth and bloody claws.
The servants returned to Primislao
and told him they had left me for dead.
But Heaven took pity
on my misfortune and my innocence.
It made the beasts lie down   110
tame and humble at my feet,
fawning over me
and comforting me in my sorrows.
I gathered my courage
and followed the beasts to their caves,
where they fed me the fruits of the forest.
Later, they brought me the hides of sheep,
goats, and other animals from the village
to make these clothes.
Then I went down the mountain   120
to find people and ask for bread.
The shepherds, who had never seen
a beast like me, ran away in fear.
One afternoon, I surprised a villager
by the banks of the stream
that waters this grove.
I forced him to tell me the news:
my husband, the king, had married my sister.

---

ted by Scylla's treachery and abandons her after he defeats her father, foreshadowing Faustina's eventual comeuppance after her seemingly successful schemes against her sister in this play.

	Forgive me, I can't go on.	
	My tears get in the way.	130

LAURO Your eyes have good reason
to shed those beautiful pearls
amid such a sea of sorrows.
But go on with your story…

TEODOSIA Faustina happily gave birth
two or three times—
always on the same date
that I was thrown to the beasts—
but the babes never lived beyond a year.
And may it always be so,   140
for she is now with child once more,
and it is predicted to be a boy.

LAURO Do not cry, my lady!
This sorrow will bring your life to an end
before you can avenge yourself
upon your cruel sister.
Such insults must offend the very heavens.
They have certainly heard your complaints,
for they have brought me here on the hunt
and given me the courage to follow you,   150
even though not a soul in this land
dares to come within a league of your cave.
I beg you, come live with me in my house.
It is not far from this grove.
If you must remain far from human society
so no one can find you,
you would be better off in my house,
where only my servants will see you.
My parents—may they rest in peace—
left me jewels and silks   160
that I would be honored to offer you now.

| | There you can recover from the years
you've spent sleeping on hides,
drinking brackish water,
and eating wild grass.
What do you say to that? | |
|---|---|---|

TEODOSIA   I can't, for my cruel fortune,
           which has condemned me to such grief,
           will surely reveal to the king
           and that tyrant queen, my sister,   170
           that I am still alive, although in this unhappy state.
           No. Allow me to carry on with this life
           which habit has made bearable
           and which I cling to in spite of it all.
           And, as you are noble, give me your word
           you will tell no one that I am Teodosia.

LAURO   I could never be so inhuman.
           I only ask to see you and serve you.

TEODOSIA   You may visit my cave whenever you wish,
           but make sure you come alone.   180
           Tell me your name.

LAURO   Lauro.

TEODOSIA   A fitting name,
           for your laurel branches
           will shelter me from the storm.

LAURO   I hear people coming.
           You follow this stream to safety,
           and I'll lead them away through the fields.

TEODOSIA   May heaven keep you, Lauro.

LAURO   And may heaven return   190
              your husband to your arms, Teodosia,
              and your crown to your head.

TEODOSIA   I hope so,
              though vengeance is best left up to God,
              for those who seek to right their own wrongs
              never come to a good end.

              Exit LAURO *and* TEODOSIA

SCENE 2

Enter SELVAGIO *and* BARTOLO, *town officials, and* LLORENTE
and BENITO, *villagers*

SELVAGIO   Everyone take a seat
              so we can start the council meeting.

BARTOLO   Let the crier call everyone to their seats
              following the order of precedence.   200
              The royal court has nothing on us—
              we know how to run a meeting properly
              and serve the interests of the people.

SELVAGIO   Llorente, take this seat.

LLORENTE   I take that as an honor.

SELVAGIO   You can sit by my side,
              not only because you are an alderman,
              but also because I'm fond of you.

BARTOLO   Benito, you take your seat as well.

BENITO   Anywhere will be fine for me: 210
                  let the meeting begin.

SELVAGIO   First, I propose we bring a doctor here—
                  on a proper salary, of course—
                  so our wives don't have to haul
                  our chamber pots to the city
                  every time we're sick.
                  Sending them all the way there
                  costs more than it would
                  just to hire a town doctor.
                  Since you can't check a pulse at a distance,   220
                  and the urine pots don't travel well,
                  we should have a doctor right here
                  to do his healing face to face,
                  because trying to cure a sick person
                  without even seeing them
                  is like sentencing a criminal
                  who has already skipped town.

BARTOLO   Selvagio is right:
                  let a doctor be found.

LLORENTE   I second the motion.   230

BENITO   Let it be done without delay,
                  for a town doctor
                  is the best judge in matters of health,
                  even if people get sick of him.
                  He can whip us into shape.

BARTOLO   We should also have
                  a dancing master in town,
                  since we do hold dances
                  every once in a while.

| LLORENTE | By my faith, you are right. 240
And speaking of dances,
since you celebrate the holy days
with such devotion,
what do we have planned this time? |

| SELVAGIO | We'll have one of those religious plays.[4]
You know how people love those. |

| BENITO | Who can write it? |

| SELVAGIO | The barber.
You know he was only a hair away
from getting his degree. 250 |

| LLORENTE | Then let's fetch him! |

| BARTOLO | (*Calling offstage*) Town crier,
go call the barber now! |

| SELVAGIO | We've had better years, you know,
since we started putting on plays. |

| BENITO | Well, let's make this a good one then.
I'll do my part to help with the expenses. |

Enter the BARBER *and* TOWN CRIER

| BARBER | And the aldermen too? |

| TOWN CRIER | They all wanted to see you. |

| BARTOLO | God save your graces. 260 |

---

4   *Autos sacramentales* were a form of popular religious play in early modern Spain, connected to celebrations of the feast of Corpus Christi. Playwrights known for *comedia* often also wrote *autos*, including Lope.

BENITO	Hail our great bloodletter,
	whose accuracy and skill
	is worthy of the Great Turk himself![5]
	How goes it with the Muses—
	are you bleeding them dry?
BARBER	It's hard to find
	the vein of verse most days.
	I'm bleeding them,
	but ever so slowly.
SELVAGIO	And how about plays? 270
BARBER	I'm not doing those anymore.
SELVAGIO	Why?
BARBER	Because I swore I wouldn't,
	and I'm going to fulfill that vow.
	If you want a simple story
	of a lady and her lover
	on a straight and narrow path,
	that I can do.
	But as for religious stuff,
	so lofty and sublime, 280
	it confuses everyone.
	So I'm all done with that,
	both in verse and in prose.
	And as for the love stories,
	I won't do those much longer either.
	I don't want people getting on my case.
	I was the first in Hungary
	to write plays in the modern style—

---

5   In this period, people went to barbers for some medical procedures, such as bloodletting, as well as grooming. The barber plays on this mock heroic title in his reply. The "Great Turk" was a term for the ruler of the Ottoman Empire.

they had them before,
but they were so old-fashioned.[6]
By schooling them all in my new style,
I've cultivated a thousand imitators
who now offer up the fruit of their labors,
though they're not the flower of the age.
It's difficult to please an entire village,
especially when the ignorant
are so eager to criticize.
I don't want a job
that requires pleasing everyone
when I could just play it safe.
There are people here
—especially the would-be poets—
who think the best way to be witty
is to nitpick my wit.
As for me, I will buy some spectacles
so I can look wise,
and curl my lip,
and scowl at the critics.
I know how to honor those
who are good to me,
praising them on the page
as in my heart.
But to those who don't appreciate me,
I say: beware!
I will lay down my pen
as others lay down their swords.

SELVAGIO   By God, you have a point!
You can't be a prophet
in your own country.

BARTOLO   Truly, a tiger treats its cubs more gently.

---

6   Lope introduces a self-referential wink, since he himself was known for pioneering a new style of playwriting.

LLORENTE	For the sake of those who love you, forgive those who speak against you. They'll come around soon enough. It's no use railing against the ways of the world.
BARBER	The Muses will vouch for me: they know my goal is always to please the wise and the learned.
BARTOLO	Will you write me a thousand sonnets?
BARBER	A thousand?
BARTOLO	I want to send them to the king.
BARBER	He has better poets at court, and they never give peasants a chance, but I'll take a stab at it.
BARTOLO	When can you have them ready?
BARBER	Within an hour.
LLORENTE	An hour?
BARBER	Just give me a few minutes.
BENITO	That's not possible! I've heard it said that poets labor, sweat, groan, moan, and perspire, just as if they were giving birth. And if they start a sonnet on Christmas, they only finish it by midsummer, and even then they're not satisfied.

BARBER	They lack the natural talent
	that Heaven gives to those it favors.
PASCUAL	(*From offstage*) I don't care what they say,
	I'm going in.
TOWN CRIER	Wait, Pascual!

Enter PASCUAL, *peasant*

PASCUAL	I will not wait.
SELVAGIO	Who is it?
PASCUAL	Me, and I bring such good news
	that you will all owe me a reward.
SELVAGIO	And I'll pay it before it's owed.
	We mustn't be ungrateful.
PASCUAL	The king is coming to hunt
	in our woods today!
	And I think Faustina will be with him,
	even though she's so close to giving birth.
SELVAGIO	Faustina!
	May she burn in Hell, amen.
	She was the reason
	for the queen's unjust death.[7]
PASCUAL	Never mind that.
	This is a great opportunity!
	The king brings so many huntsmen and hounds.

---

[7] This animosity toward Faustina is somewhat surprising from a town official like Selvagio, a sign of the common folk's continuing loyalty to Teodosia, whom he still calls "queen" instead of Faustina.

| | You must speak to him
| | and get them to kill the beast.
| | Then the threat to our village 370
| | and all the surrounding mountains
| | will come to an end.

BENITO   Just yesterday, Lorenza,
           the pretty baker girl,
           was carrying a load of bread
           when the beast surprised her on the road.
           She fled and left the bread behind.
           Later that day, Silván came along
           and looked everywhere,
           but couldn't find a thing. 380
           All the bread was gone,
           and the sack, and the saddle,
           and the donkey to boot.

BARTOLO   We can't take this any longer.
           We must speak to the king.

BENITO   Who will go?

SELVAGIO   Is the king nearby now?

PASCUAL   He's very close.

SELVAGIO   Let's go together,
           or I might lose my nerve. 390

LLORENTE   And what if you do?

BARBER   You'd better have a plan.

SELVAGIO   You must advise us,
           as a learned man.

BARBER	Let's go, and I'll tell you what you must do: you must be clear but concise, brief but thorough.
BARTOLO	Today that beast will die.
BENITO	I'd give everything I own 400 to see it dead at last!

Exit all

SCENE 3

Enter FAUSTINA *on a litter, and* PRIMISLAO, *the king of Hungary, on horseback, accompanied by much fanfare, through a ceremonial entrance, and some* HUNTSMEN *with dogs on leashes and others with falcons.* FAUSTINA *and* PRIMISLAO *dismount*

HUNTSMAN	These sweet and pleasant airs will give respite to weary travelers. The wind stirs the clear waters of a spring, so lovely it would beguile Narcissus, framed by juniper and chestnut trees.[8]
FAUSTINA	This whole meadow is a paradise, a canvas where nature shows its artful hand.
PRIMISLAO	My love, before you venture further up this steep mountain, 410

---

8   *Narcissus*: A beautiful Greek youth who fell in love with his own reflection, doomed to pine away for an image he could never reach. This scene starts in a high poetic register—a brief romantic interlude before sorrow catches up to Faustina and Primislao, who have shown some narcissistic tendencies of their own in their treatment of Teodosia.

	rest here in its verdant lap
	and let its meadow honor your beauty.
	Behold its crown of silver snow above,
	melting into emerald pastures below.
	Behold the shade of a thousand lofty trees,
	and springs that long to mirror your beauty.
	While the birds sing in unison
	a fine harmony of love,
	the waters, envious of their melody,
	babble their own sweet song. 420
	Then the valley echoes in response.
	Behold this lovely lane of willows
	and this meadow,
	where every flower can be found:
	here the lilies release their divine aroma;
	there grows the hyacinth, the violet, the jasmine,
	and the blood-red rose.
	Rest here, dear wife,
	so that you may continue up the mountain
	when the heat of the day subsides. 430

FAUSTINA   The comforting embrace of this meadow
           cannot replace yours, my king,
           nor can all the treasures of the earth.
           Without the joys of your love,
           neither this idyllic place
           nor its cool crystalline spring
           are worth anything at all.
           But with you here, it is bliss.

PRIMISLAO May the heavens grant you a long life,
           my Faustina, for I can find no delight   440
           away from your beauty.
           It gives me life, nourishes my soul,
           turns war into peace,
           and trials into glory.

Enter SELVAGIO, BARTOLO, *and* LLORENTE *to the side*

SELVAGIO   Approach with care.

BARTOLO   Did you memorize your speech?

SELVAGIO   I studied it well,
            but I'm drawing a blank
            now that I see the king.

PRIMISLAO   Who are they?   450

HUNTSMAN   Peasants from the village, my lord.

SELVAGIO, BARTOLO *and* LLORENTE *approach* PRIMISLAO
                and FAUSTINA

SELVAGIO   Listen to us, I pray.

PRIMISLAO   (*Aside to* FAUSTINA) "You bray" is more like it.

FAUSTINA   (*Aside to* PRIMISLAO) Well put.

SELVAGIO   I pray, my lord,
            will you help us kill a beast
            that eats up our crops?
            I pray, my lady,
            will you grant us your favor?
            The animal dwells in these woods, my lord,   460
            and it is so strong it steals all our food.
            By taking its life away,
            you'll give ours back,
            and when you wage your next war,
            we'll fight for you wherever you go.

PRIMISLAO   (*Aside*) This village is full of braying asses,

	and the forest of roaring monsters.	
	(*Aloud*) It's long been said that a beast lives	
	in the thick of these woods.	
BARTOLO	Its fame has spread abroad,	470
	in print and in song.	
PRIMISLAO	Then why have you not killed it yet?	
BARTOLO	This place is very low on spears and horses,	
	and it's not as if the beast	
	doesn't know how to defend itself.	
	It's more like you	
	than like a helpless animal.	
	It knows how to run and speak,	
	and even how to force itself on maidens.	
PRIMISLAO	Maidens?	480
BARTOLO	Yes, I could name more than six	
	—unless they're lying.[9]	
PRIMISLAO	What shape does it take?	
SELVAGIO	I tremble to describe it.	
	It's...like a person,	
	more or less.	
PRIMISLAO	How helpful.	
	And does it speak, too?	
BARTOLO	Yes.	
PRIMISLAO	Is it strong?	490

---

9   A joke about the maidens possibly using the beast as an excuse for their own secret trysts in the woods.

BARTOLO   None can conquer it.
          Let's see... It has a face in the front,
          a back in the back,
          and a body like a giant.

PRIMISLAO Enough, you've frightened the queen.

FAUSTINA   It's not the beast that frightens me,
           but this heat and this sudden pain I feel.

HUNTSMAN   This meadow is not as cool
           as those woods over there, my lord.

FAUSTINA   Oh, God in heaven!   500
           What is this I'm feeling?

PRIMISLAO If it is cooler in the woods,
           you should rest there, my Faustina.

SELVAGIO   Follow me, my lord.
           I know the way through the thicket.
           There the stream barely trickles
           through cattails and rushes,
           while thick brambles and hanging vines
           make a thousand wild snares.

PRIMISLAO (*To the* HUNTSMAN) Go station yourself   510
           in the shade of that wood
           while my wife rests,
           and once the sun gives some respite
           from the heat of the afternoon,
           meet us at the spring in that wild grove
           and we'll see if we can find this beast—

FAUSTINA   The pain is getting worse...

PRIMISLAO	—for it will not get away,
	no, not even if it has wings!

Exit PRIMISLAO, BARTOLO *and* SELVAGIO *in one direction,*
FAUSTINA *and the* HUNTSMAN *in the other direction, until only*
LLORENTE *remains*

LLORENTE	The queen will wait by the stream	520
	while the heat of the day abates,	
	for the sun's rays are too strong for her now.	
	Oh, if only those rays would strike you down,	
	tyrant Faustina, unjust and fierce as you are,	
	far worse than the beast	
	which shelters in the woods	
	and stalks our land.	
	It is just an animal in search of food,	
	while you are an unjust woman	
	whose tyrannical plots	530
	have caused us so much grief.	
	You doomed the beautiful Teodosia,	
	the king's wife—she was holy, honest,	
	and adored throughout Hungary,	
	and your beloved sister, no less.	
	She has become a martyr to us all now,	
	much good that does her!	
	What are those shouts?	
	There goes a boar,	
	with the king and his huntsmen	540
	giving chase at full speed.	
	But heavens, what is this?	
	Is this the beast feared throughout Hungary?	

Enter TEODOSIA

TEODOSIA	Stop!

LLORENTE   Oh no!

TEODOSIA   Do not be afraid, my good man.
             Trust me, I'm not here to hurt you.

LLORENTE   I beg of you, my lord,
             for God's sake have pity on me!
             (*Aside*) Those eyes burn like fire! 550

TEODOSIA   Get a hold of yourself
             and listen to me!

LLORENTE   (*Aloud*) And then will you let me go?

TEODOSIA   As soon as you've heard me out.

LLORENTE   What do you want?

TEODOSIA   Just to know who those people are.

LLORENTE   I fear you won't like my answer.

TEODOSIA   Why not?

LLORENTE   It's the king, and that tyrant
             who was sister to Teodosia. 560
             Like the goddess Diana,
             she wants to make you into another Actaeon,
             the hunter turned into prey.[10]
             The peasants who live here have told them
             about all you have stolen and devoured,
             and they've sworn to kill you.

---

10   *Actaeon*: In myth, a human hunter who came upon the goddess Diana, an avowed virgin, and dared to spy on her as she bathed in the woods. As punishment, she transformed him into a stag and his own hounds killed him.

TEODOSIA	This is not the first time they've attempted as much.
LLORENTE	You don't seem as beastly as they say in the village. 570
TEODOSIA	But I am a beast, forced to live and die among the animals.
LLORENTE	Then hide, on your life! They're out to kill you—
TEODOSIA	Heaven will spare me.
LLORENTE	They will lie in wait for you along this verdant riverbank. But, as for me, now that I've seen you, I am no longer afraid, 580 and instead grow fond of your face, lovelier than the evening star. Where do you live? (*Sees she is taken aback*) Just so I can bring you bread and wine to ease your sorrows.
TEODOSIA	The woods house me and the good earth shelters me. Go now, and tell no one that you have seen me.
LLORENTE	I will tell no one, 590 not even the trees or the mountain springs! God keep you from all traitors!
TEODOSIA	Alas, even your own blood can betray you.

LLORENTE	Oh fields, flowers, springs:
	the one you call a beast
	should be crowned the god of love!

Exit LLORENTE

TEODOSIA	Oh rugged mountain so very high,	
	like an Icarus reaching for the sky,	
	raised up by the ambitious earth,	600
	the sun's beauty to attempt.	
	Yet it melts your wings of driven snow,	
	scattering them like feathers below.[11]	
	In the meadow they lie on riverbeds,	
	and in a deep lake come to rest.	
	For years I've lived as your human beast,	
	yet those who tried to kill me once	
	have now embarked on a new attempt.	
	Heaven and Earth keep me in your care.	
	How sad I'd be if I did not know well	610
	that all our grief must end with our death.	

Enter FAUSTINA *with a baby in her arms*

FAUSTINA	Who has ever borne such suffering,	
	all alone like this?	
	Some dark fate brought me to these woods.	
	No sooner had we arrived	
	than the king ran off to chase a boar,	
	leaving me to fend for myself.	
	When I first heard them mention this beast,	
	—oh scourge of Hungary!—	
	I was struck to the heart.	620
	Once alone, I fell into a dead faint	

---

11 *Icarus*: Son of the inventor Daedalus, who gave him wings made of wax and warned him not to fly too close to the sun, lest they melt. Icarus did not listen and tragically fell to his death, becoming a symbol of foolish ambition.

on the grassy meadow.
Now I awake to find the fruit of my womb
amid the reeds and the cattails,
this poor cursed child.
I must swaddle her as best I can,
lest the beast come down to the water,
as they say it often does.
I must find my husband now,
or the beast will take the babe   630
from my belly into its own.
Yet I dare not call out for help,
since I fear that would attract
the cruel monster.

TEODOSIA   (*Aside*) That is my sister, my enemy!
It's Faustina! Can this be?
Can it be you I see in this wilderness,
oh inhuman creature?
Heaven must have brought you here
so that I may take my revenge on you.   640
Since you once denied me,
your own flesh and blood,
may you never enjoy the babe born unto you.
Not in vain did Heaven bring you
to this harsh place in which I live.
You betrayed me once,
and now seeing your suffering
lessens my own.
She may recognize me—
I will hide my face with my hair.   650
(*Aloud*) Behold, I am here.

FAUSTINA   Oh heavens!
This is the end!
Oh my king, my lord,
will no one protect me?

                    FAUSTINA *faints*

TEODOSIA   Did she faint at the sight of me,
           or has Heaven finally made her confront
           how she took my life from me,
           along with my kingdom and my honor?
           A perfect opportunity for revenge   660
           ... if my noble nature allows it.
           If they have made a beast of me,
           then a fierce beast I shall be!
           But no... I am still a woman,
           and so I must remain.
           My only revenge,
           which Heaven will smile on,
           will be to take the ill-begotten fruit of her womb
           on which she places all her hopes.
           She will reap no joy from this birth.   670
           Savage beast, cruel murderer,
           I will not take the babe's life,
           but will remove it from your sight
           to quell the great anger that plagues me still.
           I will make the babe into a beast like me,
           so that I may have some company
           and a witness to my pain
           for as long as I live.
           You will never see this little one again,
           and may Heaven never give you another.   680
           May it also someday free me
           from this beastly life and my suffering,
           as one who once enjoyed a happier state.

                    TEODOSIA *takes the baby*

           People are coming.
           I must retreat to the mountains
           before they get any closer.

                    My cave among the rocks
                    is safe from the king.

HUNTSMAN   (*Offstage*) This way!
                    The queen is gone!   690

TEODOSIA   May Heaven give me strength!

Exit TEODOSIA, *then* PRIMISLAO *and his men enter*

PRIMISLAO   Oh no!
                    Search the mountain, men!

HUNTSMAN   The horses won't make it up there!

PRIMISLAO   I have lost my greatest treasure!

HUNTSMAN   There's something on the ground over there!

PRIMISLAO   If that is the queen, she must surely be dead.

HUNTSMAN   It is her.

                    PRIMISLAO *goes to* FAUSTINA

PRIMISLAO   Am I seeing things?
                    Wake up, my love.   700
                    See how I bathe your face
                    with these loving tears.

FAUSTINA   (*Waking*) Who is there?

PRIMISLAO   Oh sweet gods above,
                    give her breath, give her life.
                    Did she faint, or was she wounded?

HUNTSMAN   Both, I think.

PRIMISLAO   My Faustina!

FAUSTINA   My lord!

PRIMISLAO   What's wrong?   710

FAUSTINA   A terrible thing has happened.
           That fierce beast—

PRIMISLAO   (*Aside*) It was madness to leave her side.

FAUSTINA   —it came from beyond the river
           and attacked me,
           looming above me like a giant.
           Then it grabbed the fruit of my womb
           and took off for the mountains,
           like a wild Titan.[12]
           For as soon as you left,   720
           our babe was born—
           you might find some consolation
           in the fact that it was only a girl in the end.

PRIMISLAO   What great misfortune!
           Why, oh angry heavens,
           may none of our children live?
           (*To* FAUSTINA) But since you have been spared,
           let us see to you now.

FAUSTINA   (*Aside*) I do not dare tell him
           that I deserve all this misfortune and more.   730

PRIMISLAO   Huntsmen, the beast has taken my daughter!

---

12   *Titan*: One of the gods who ruled the cosmos before the Olympians, often depicted as giants.

> If it has killed the babe, it must be killed.
> After it, everyone!
> Whoever first finds it and kills it
> will be rewarded with lands
> as far as their eyes can see.

HUNTSMAN You will soon see it dead.

PRIMISLAO Godspeed.

Exit HUNTSMAN *and the other men, leaving* PRIMISLAO *and* FAUSTINA *alone*

> Courage, my dear wife,
> show some spirit.   740

FAUSTINA How can I bear this?
I'm not sure I can survive it.

PRIMISLAO All our mortal joys
thus come to a sad end.
I promise whoever manages
to defeat this savage beast
will be rewarded with my crown itself.

Exit all

SCENE 4

PLÁCIDO (*From offstage*) Get the boat to shore!

FULGENCIO (*From offstage*) None of the sailors must come with us, Arfindo.

ARFINDO (*From offstage*) Everyone stay on the boat!   750

PLÁCIDO   (*From offstage*) Stay back!
                None must see this place.

FULGENCIO   (*From offstage*) Bring the boat ashore!

Enter three gentlemen, PLÁCIDO, FULGENCIO, *and* ARFINDO,
with FELIPE, *a young boy, as though alighting from a boat. The men
speak apart from the boy*

ARFINDO   What island is this?

PLÁCIDO   Truth be told,
                I do not know if it is an island at all.

FULGENCIO   We are so far from Spain in any case,
                what difference does it make?

ARFINDO   It might make a difference to know
                where we are leaving this innocent child.   760

FULGENCIO   It makes little difference, Arfindo.
                He will be a morsel for the beasts
                and vultures in this deserted place.
                Let us leave him, then,
                and may Heaven forgive our grave sin.

ARFINDO   Fulgencio, I only do as the count commands,
                for he is my master.
                His daughter was disobedient and insolent,
                guilty of marrying her own cousin in secret.
                I'm sure he'll put them both to death.   770
                And as for this child, his grandson,
                the count has condemned him to a distant death,
                or at least a life far from Barcelona and all of Spain.
                Here no one will ever know
                that he is the count's grandson,

| | even if Fortune keeps him safe, |
| | which will never happen in these woods. |

PLÁCIDO   God could make it so.
            There is no fortune, no destiny, no occurrence
            that does not hang, live, and rely   780
            on His divine will.

ARFINDO   The count is more of a barbarian
            than a father to his daughter.
            Where is the sense in imprisoning
            this young boy's father, his own nephew,
            the second son of the king of Naples?

FULGENCIO   Reason no longer rules as it should.
            The count's desire for revenge
            overcomes the obligations of flesh and blood.
            He said if the crime had lasted only a month or a year   790
            he would have been more inclined to mercy,
            but see the age of the child we've brought here!
            Given the continued deceit,
            he wants the lovers to die in chains,
            and the child to be abandoned in a strange land.

PLÁCIDO   I suspect this land is strange enough:
            untamed woods and steep terrain,
            narrow straits and shallow streams,
            unyielding oaks and somber beeches,
            crowned chestnuts and lofty pines,   800
            gloomy cypresses and thick brambles—
            there's no path in sight.
            (*To* FELIPE) Wait here.
            We're just going to hunt in these woods
            for some deer or boar to eat
            on the voyage home to Barcelona.

FELIPE   Why must I wait here?
              Shouldn't I come with you?

ARFINDO   We're going very far,
              and Plácido wants us to go alone.   810
              You will only get tired, my dear.
              Just wait in this meadow until we return.
              You can sit and rest here.
              Play with the flowers that adorn this stream—
              they're just like you,
              so rosy and fresh!
              Sit here among the grasses
              and pick yellow lilies,
              or throw rocks at the birds
              through those brambles there.   820
              And if we take too long, my sweet,
              you can take a little nap.

FELIPE   Don't try to fool me,
              that just makes me even angrier.
              Tell me the truth, friends:
              if you are leaving me
              because my wicked grandfather intends
              to let me die in this wild place,
              just drop this ruse and kill me now,
              so you can reassure him   830
              that his evil deeds have been done.
              The sooner I die,
              the sooner I will ask the Lord for revenge.

FULGENCIO   Oh God!
              What lion or fierce tiger could be so cruel?
              My eyes are swimming with tears.

ARFINDO   If you pay so much heed
              to his innocence and piety,

	you will never find the heart
	to execute the count's command, 840
	whether just or unjust.

FULGENCIO Felipe, stay here.
If you get hungry,
see all these treats I've brought you
on this cloth here,
so tasty and sweet.

FELIPE Can't I come with you?

ARFINDO You'll just get tired.

FELIPE I won't.

ARFINDO Oh yes you will. 850
This wilderness is full of crags and peaks.
God be with you, God keep you!

FELIPE Don't take too long…

FULGENCIO (*Aside*) His tender words would melt a heart of stone.

ARFINDO Let's go, my lords.

Exit ARFINDO, FULGENCIO, *and* PLÁCIDO

FELIPE How could they abandon me
in such a lonely place?
I'm sure they'll sail off now
and leave me to die.
I saw tears of pity in their eyes. 860
I'm going to climb that rock
and look out to sea.

FELIPE *climbs a rock as* LAURO, LLORENTE, *and* BENITO *enter below*

LLORENTE   There will be a big reward
           for whoever finds the beast.

LAURO   There's little chance of that:
           this is very harsh terrain,
           though full of prey.
           (*Aside*) I would hate to see them find the queen,
           though at least she would die avenged,
           having stolen what they say   870
           Faustina birthed in these woods.

FELIPE   (*Above*) What's this I see?
           Poor me, how was I born so unlucky?
           Their boat is already far from shore.
           Now they're boarding the ship,
           now they're hoisting the sails,
           and they have a favorable wind.
           This is what my grandfather intended
           when he imprisoned my parents.
           Woe is me, what will I do   880
           all alone in this wilderness?

LAURO   (*Aloud*) Oh heavens!
           Do you hear a tender voice
           coming from those trees?

BENITO   Perhaps it is a bird
           singing to the sun above?

FELIPE   Woe is me, what am I to do
           in this strange land?

LLORENTE   Is it a spring that murmurs

	and weeps so sadly?	890
LAURO	No, it's not a bird or a spring. I think it's a human voice. Don't you hear the crying, getting louder?	
FELIPE	What did I do to offend my grandfather? Oh God, I hear beasts in those bushes! Have mercy, oh Heaven above, they are coming to eat me!	
LAURO	Wait! I think I see the source of all that weeping.	900
BENITO	I can't see anything.	
LAURO	Can't you see that little boy up there, crying on that boulder?	
BENITO	You're right!	
LLORENTE	He could move the very stones to mercy.	
BENITO	And dressed so finely to boot.	
LAURO	(*Shouting to* FELIPE) May God protect you, child. Come down and tell us what has befallen you.	
FELIPE	Don't kill me, gentlemen! I've come from a far-off land.	910
LAURO	By God, he speaks Spanish!	
LLORENTE	(*To* LAURO) Maybe you can understand what he says,

	since you've been to Spain.
LAURO	Yes, I spent three years there.[13] Come here, child, come down! Don't be afraid!
FELIPE	Are you Christians?
LAURO	Can't you tell by our dress and manners?
FELIPE	So you're not Moors?
LAURO	No, more boorish than Moorish.
FELIPE	Are you going to hurt me?
LAURO	Of course not!
FELIPE	Well then, I'll come down!
LAURO	(*Aside*) How strange, what could this all mean?

FELIPE joins the men below

FELIPE	Please don't hurt me, my lords.
LAURO	What are you doing on this mountain, when you sound and look like a Spaniard?
FELIPE	Well, sir...
LAURO	Go on.

---

13   Lauro and Felipe proceed to talk in Spanish, which the other men do not understand and thus do not hear about Felipe's true heritage.

FELIPE	The count of Barcelona
has a daughter, and I am her son.
My father is a nobleman,
son to the king of a land beyond the sea.
He never properly wed my mother
and when my grandfather found out,
he had her detained
and me sent away on a ship.   940
I was to be abandoned on some island
or wilderness far from Spain,
so he would not bloody his hands
by taking such a tender life.
What land is this?
LAURO	Hungary.
FELIPE	Tell me: in Hungary,
do they kill little boys
who are unloved by their grandfathers?
LAURO	Such innocence! 950
No, my lord, goodness no.
We spoil them with treats and toys.
We give them clothes and a bed,
and breakfast, lunch, and dinner too.
Come, I'll look after you
as your own mother would.
The grandson of a prince deserves
to be treated accordingly.
God willing, the day will come
when the count will feel remorse   960
for what he did to you.
Then he will search for you,
care for you once more,
and claim you as his heir.

FELIPE	God, I hope so! Then I would pay you back a thousand-fold. Is your house nearby?
LAURO	Just beyond those rocks.
FELIPE	And are there other children there?
LAURO	There is one about your age, my dear. 970
FELIPE	And does he go to school?
LAURO	No, my little lord. The village is too far from my house.
FELIPE	Then I will teach him how to read.
LAURO	Reading's all well and good, but it would be better if you taught him how to bear arms. Kings reward those who serve them with their swords.
FELIPE	Maybe when kings get to rule, 980 but not when they've been exiled.
LAURO	What a clever boy!
LLORENTE	(*To* LAURO) What did he say to you? We can't understand his language.
LAURO	Strange and novel things that you'll understand someday. (*To* FELIPE) Come, my dear, and meet the one who will be your mother until you are reunited with your own.

FELIPE	I will honor her	990
	as my lady and my aunt.	

LAURO   May the heavens restore you
        to your crown in Naples and Barcelona.
        What is your name?

FELIPE Felipe.

LAURO   Felipe, a fine name.
        If you're anything like Felipe of Macedon,
        you'll beget another Alexander
        to rule the world.[14]
        What is that you have there?   1000

FELIPE Some food left for me by those men
        who sailed off without me.

LAURO   You will fare better here.
        Come along, my dear,
        let us leave these woods.
        God has brought you to my house
        so you may one day be a king.

End of ACT I

---

14   Referring to Felipe, or Philip, a historical ruler of Macedon and father of Alexander the Great, who shares a name with Spain's king at the time.

ACT II

SCENE 1

Twenty years later

Enter TEODOSIA *and* ROSAURA, *now a young woman, both dressed in hides*

TEODOSIA	Rosaura, must I always scold you
	and remind you of the dangers you'll encounter
	if you dare to leave this place? 1010
	Can't you see that I'm trying to protect you?
	Why am I always finding you
	in such thorny situations?
	Remember—we are two animals,
	hunted by men with their hidden weapons.
	If you leave, they will take us as prey or kill us.
	How could you think it safe to leave
	when there might be no way back?
ROSAURA	Mother, who could possibly resist
	the desire to know?[15] 1020
	When I was a little girl,
	I would heed your lessons

---

15   Throughout this scene Rosaura shows intelligence and the ability to reason philosophically (much to Teodosia's chagrin), though she has been raised "in a state of nature" away from the rest of humanity.

and I understood your warnings.
Now that I am older,
my own nature rebels against their harshness
and I no longer wish to obey.
Tell me, what's that we see up there?

TEODOSIA   The heavens where dwells the Creator
of everything that is, was, and will be.

ROSAURA   Didn't you say, 1030
when you were teaching me your faith,
that He created all creatures?

TEODOSIA   Yes, I did say that.

ROSAURA   And didn't you say that He made a man
by the name of Adam?

TEODOSIA   Yes, just like a sculptor,
the Creator melds and shapes figures:
thus, He created man.

ROSAURA   And once made,
didn't you say He made a woman from Adam's rib 1040
and commanded the two be as one flesh?

TEODOSIA   Yes, because God made them
in order to multiply the human race.

ROSAURA   Yes, yes, so you said—
in His eternal wisdom,
so the earth would overflow
with their blessed offspring.
You've told me that all other living things,
whether in the meadow or the mountains,
are called animals, 1050

| | and only man turns his face to Heaven, |
| | where he belongs. |

TEODOSIA   That's right,
            only man does that.

ROSAURA   If that's so, then how can you say
            that the two of us are beasts
            when you praise and bless God?
            Don't you see the contradiction?
            If you call me an animal,
            how can you then tell me   1060
            that I belong to Heaven,
            or that this body
            holds an immortal soul?
            If I have a soul,
            and it is destined for Heaven,
            then I cannot be a beast.

TEODOSIA   You are a beast
            because you are treated as one,
            cruelly hunted by men
            wherever you roam.   1070

ROSAURA   That's just it!
            If women were created
            to keep men company,
            why, then, do men hunt
            those they are meant to love?

TEODOSIA   You are not a woman.

ROSAURA   Then what am I?

TEODOSIA   You're not what you once were.

ROSAURA   But who created me?
          According to your faith, 1080
          I was not born a mere plant
          because I have a soul
          that elevates my thoughts to Heaven.

TEODOSIA These woods, this snow, this ice—
          they created you.

ROSAURA   That's nonsense.
          The woods can only make trees, fruits, and flowers,
          and the snow can do no more than freeze.

TEODOSIA And what of these deer running by,
          and those birds flying above? 1090
          Weren't they created by these woods?

ROSAURA   No, for the bird flies on the wind,
          despite being born on land.
          What you're saying makes no sense.
          I am not a bird, that much is clear:
          I can't fly and I can speak.

TEODOSIA You are mistaken.

ROSAURA   Why do you say that?

TEODOSIA Birds have a language too,
          and I can understand it. 1100

ROSAURA   You?

TEODOSIA Me.

ROSAURA   Oh?
          Then tell me what the nightingale just said.

TEODOSIA   She sings her husband's praises.

ROSAURA   Actually, she said:
             love comes naturally!

TEODOSIA   How do you know that
             if you don't speak the language of birds?

ROSAURA   No, really, how do you know?   1110
             There's no way you understand
             the cries of those small birds.
             They're nothing like my voice.
             If you understand their speech,
             you must be a bird too,
             and maybe I'm not like you after all.

TEODOSIA   Enough of your backtalk!

ROSAURA   Mother, don't be angry
             at my desire to know.

TEODOSIA   Beasts must be seen and not heard.   1120
             They needn't understand,
             nor argue, nor question.

ROSAURA   If I am a beast…
             every beast I see has a mate by its side.
             The deer along these banks
             have begotten children with their deer husbands.
             That's how those fawns happened, mother.
             If I am a beast, as you say,
             then tell me: what beast did you lie with
             so that I might be born in your image   1130
             and with an immortal soul?
             Tell me who my father is.

TEODOSIA	I was both your mother and your father.
ROSAURA	That, mother, is nonsense.
TEODOSIA	Mother of pearl engenders its child from dew. The beautiful shell opens at dawn to let the sun in. That same sun creates humans, and they are shaped by the star under which they are born.[16]
ROSAURA	That may be so, mother, but that doesn't explain the rest of it. If only the sun were involved, one sun would bear another sun. It's clear that's not it. The sun must take matter from somewhere. I don't deny it plays a role, but to make one like me requires another me. The sun warms the one who created me.[17]
TEODOSIA	That's what I said, Rosaura: when the sun came to me, then you came to be.
ROSAURA	Then let us praise the sun. But, mother, in case you cease to be, I'd like to have another being for company. So, tell me how and when you joined with the sun, because I want to create a being who will live under my wing

---

16   Referring to astrological signs affecting human personalities and fortunes.
17   Referring to older theories of procreation which attribute responsibility for shaping the offspring to the male.

                    as I have lived under yours.

TEODOSIA   Who is filling your head with this nonsense?

ROSAURA   Just today, mother
                —if it wasn't a trick of the light—
                I saw something that almost looked like me.
                It must have been the sun
                with whom you keep company now and then.

TEODOSIA   You saw a man?

ROSAURA   So it was a man I saw!
                I think you may be right.   1170

TEODOSIA   Oh Rosaura,
                you will be the ruin of me!

ROSAURA   I had wandered into the bushes,
                and through some brambles
                I saw him remove something
                that had covered his whole body.
                He hung it on a nearby branch
                and jumped into a spring,
                where he began to wash
                and rub himself all over.   1180
                By the time he got out and covered himself again,
                I couldn't give thanks enough
                to the mother who bore him.
                I laughed as I watched him put those things back on,
                thinking: "You were better off naked!
                Why cover yourself up?"

TEODOSIA   Enough! You make me so angry,
                I don't know how I put up with you.

ROSAURA   But mother, if he was the sun,
          and the sun is my father,   1190
          then what is the problem?

TEODOSIA That sun could burn you
          if he turned his gaze on you.

ROSAURA   Oh mother, you're right.
          Ever since I saw him,
          I have felt like I'm dying
          from this fire he lit inside me.
          I haven't been able to eat or sleep.
          I can find no peace.
          Tell me, mother: were you like this   1200
          the day you first saw the sun?

TEODOSIA What are you saying?
          You've been seeing men?

ROSAURA   Not men, just the naked sun.

TEODOSIA I will kill you
          if you leave this cave again.
          Aren't you afraid that sun
          will mistreat you
          or take you prisoner
          if he gets a hold of you?   1210

ROSAURA   Yes, I had thought of that,
          but what shall I do
          if I happen to see him again?
          Tell me what to do.

TEODOSIA He may kill you if he catches you.
          To make him flee,

	you must make the sign of the cross,	
	just like I taught you.	
ROSAURA	And then he'll flee from me?	
TEODOSIA	Yes, Rosaura.	1220
ROSAURA	Then that's what I'll do.	
TEODOSIA	Enough of this.	
	Let's go this way.	
	There's better hunting	
	at the foot of that clear stream.	
ROSAURA	Such a lovely creature, the sun.	
	It's a shame he can burn me.	

Exit TEODOSIA *and* ROSAURA

SCENE 2

Enter LAURO, *older, wearing an overcoat and carrying a walking stick;* FELIPE, *now a young man, carrying a spear; and* BELARDO, *a villager*

LAURO	You speak of such strange things.	
BELARDO	It's all true, what they say about that beast.	
	FELIPE *and* LAURO *speak apart*	
FELIPE	Father, didn't they kill the beast	1230
	—the one that used to terrorize	
	our rivers, woods, and fields?	

LAURO	It's been twenty years since they last searched for it. Not a single nook or cranny in the forest or the mountains was left untouched, so I was sure it was dead.
FELIPE	On long winter nights, an old peasant who remembered well the "Beast of Hungary" 1240 would tell tales of it around the fire. He claimed the beast was surely killed that day when Faustina, the king's new wife,[18] gave birth to a beautiful baby girl right here among the flowers of this meadow. The beast did not hurt Faustina, but fled with the baby up into the hills as the hunters gave chase.
LAURO	A terrible misfortune! Faustina has had no children since then. 1250
FELIPE	So there's no heir to the throne?
LAURO	No, Felipe, and I will tell you why: God wouldn't want to bring a child into such a terrible scheme. You are a sensible man, and descended from Spaniards, who have always been trustworthy. I will tell you the whole wicked tale, as best I can remember it.
FELIPE	Thank you for your confidence in me. 1260 I already owe you so much

---

18   Another instance of the villagers refusing to acknowledge Faustina as the current queen.

	for taking me in so long ago.

LAURO   It's been years since I found you,
           sad and alone, as the sun was setting.
           It was where that olive tree now grows,
           ...or was it a little bit further?
           There it is, that's the very boulder!
           I recognize it now.

FELIPE   May God bless you.
           You're the reason my light still burns bright   1270
           despite the many winds
           that have sought to extinguish it.

FELIPE and LAURO return to BELARDO

LAURO   (*To* BELARDO) Tell me, my friend:
           how did you come to see
           that beast in these woods?

BELARDO   What do you mean "that" beast?
           I'm telling you, sir, there were two.

LAURO   Fear must have made you see double.

BELARDO   It's true that I have never felt
           such fear as I did last night,   1280
           but I am sure there were two.

LAURO   Did they come near you?

BELARDO   Yes, but not because I was trying to be brave.
           They were chasing after me
           and when they got close,
           I jumped in the river to escape them.
           Then, you wouldn't believe

| | how the older of the two
               pelted me with rocks.

| LAURO | So it was not fear, Belardo?   1290
               You really saw two of them?

| BELARDO | Without a doubt, sir.

| FELIPE | Come now, Belardo, you were just scared.
               Tell us the truth.

| BELARDO | Unless my eyes deceived me,
               I saw two, without a doubt.
               I saw two, as beautiful as they were swift.
               Belardo doesn't tell lies!
               This brown sackcloth here covers a soul
               that prides itself on always telling the truth.   1300
               You know I never even go to the city
               because the truth is hard to find there.
               You must believe me,
               there are whole families of savages here.
               I saw them!

| FELIPE | You did?

| BELARDO | Yes, because savages always go right for me.

| FELIPE | Why?

| BELARDO | God only knows.

| LAURO | (*Aside*) I'm familiar with that older beast,   1310
               but I can't quite believe there are two of them.
               I know the older one is the rightful queen,
               and she, of all women, would remain chaste.
               But if she has given birth,

| | it is clear that I am mistaken.
The younger beast cannot be
the baby stolen from Faustina,
because I saw them bring its tiny body
to the king, all torn apart.
It must instead be the fruit   1320
of some secret love with a shepherd
and his less-than-honest embraces.
Oh loneliness,
what terrible things you lead us to! |

FELIPE   What are you saying, Lauro?

LAURO   Don't say anything in the city
            about seeing these wild savages, Belardo.

BELARDO   There are plenty of well-dressed savages
            in the court to match them.
            I do my best to stay away from such animals   1330
            —they're all lousy from head to toe.
            What I need to do now
            is warm myself up with some wine.
            I'm allergic to water, you know.

FELIPE   Will you drink it or wear it?

BELARDO   Both, if I miss my mouth.

Exit BELARDO

LAURO   Now that we are alone, my son,
            I'd like to ask you something
            that weighs on me in my old age.
            Tell me, are you not troubled   1340
            by seeing yourself in this state
            despite being the nephew of a king

                and grandson to the count of Barcelona?
                Do you not long to know how and where
                you were born and raised?
                Are you truly as happy as you seem,
                living a poor and humble life in this hut,
                barely civilized?
                Do you not miss the clothes, the food, the honor,
                that your true station would merit?   1350
                Does the nobility of your birth
                not move your soul to abhor such a crude life?
                Do you not feel the wind in your sails,
                or consider what you owe your noble courage?
                Do you not think of all that you have lost
                and of your beloved homeland,
                which lies only a short sail away?
                Set forth! Journey to Spain before my death,
                so that I may see you crowned at last.
                I raised you and now my heart longs   1360
                to see you restored to Spain.
                What do you say, oh great Felipe?

FELIPE   Oh father, this can't be the voice of love.
                If you're saying this for my own good,
                then why are you pushing me away
                with such harsh and unloving counsel?
                I don't know any princes or counts,
                and all I ask of God, dear father,
                is that you may enjoy a long life
                with me by your side.   1370
                Why, sir, do you deny me this?

LAURO   I see in you a healthy young man:
                so gallant, generous, and brave
                that Mars or Apollo might envy you.[19]

---

19   *Mars, Apollo*: Gods known for martial valor.

>   But I also see that you deserve more
>   than my poor household, Felipe.
>   I would like to see you in a worthier state.
>   You know I would give you anything,
>   but there is nothing here to give.

FELIPE   Are you worried that I'll use up   1380
>   everything you do have, Lauro?

LAURO   Oh my son, my beloved son,
>   I do not deserve such harshness.
>   You are bringing me to tears.
>   You have never been this ungrateful before.
>   This is a fault among the many virtues
>   that Heaven has bestowed upon you.

FELIPE   Oh father, dry your tears, I beg of you.
>   I spoke nonsense.
>   You seem so burdened today,   1390
>   and I would not want you to think ill
>   of the one you've raised as your son.
>   I have no use for a scepter, crown or country,
>   but I esteem you more than all the gold of the East.
>   In the end, crowns adorn nothing but fleshless skulls,
>   mocked by their royal heirs.
>   In truth, I would rather look upon
>   the faded pictures on your walls,
>   listening to your stories
>   while roasting rabbits together,   1400
>   than behold Phaeton's Palace of the Sun.
>   I care not for his chariot and horses,
>   or for a swift Pegasus to ride.[20]
>   Could there be any truer friends and servants
>   than these honest peasants around us?

---

20   *Phaeton*: Son of the Greek sun god, Helios, who begged to drive his father's chariot for one day, with tragic results. *Pegasus*: A mythical winged horse.

| | Kings themselves would envy us.
| | Here the birds make music
| | and flowers adorn our table,
| | while at court everyone speaks false praise.
| | Let the lords have their court, 1410
| | with its ceaseless cares and ambitions.
| | As for me, I'll take these restful oaks and pastures,
| | where only the streams murmur,
| | not the envious whisperers.

LAURO   Son, I know you are trying to comfort me,
        but nothing would be of greater comfort
        than for the heavens to give you your due.
        You should go to Spain.
        As your father I command it.
        Return to Spain to seek your better fortune— 1420
        perhaps its wheel has finally turned.[21]
        Find out if your beautiful mother is now free,
        and whether the count still rules
        or your father holds power now.
        Then act as your brave thoughts deem best.
        Then you can return to me,
        and, if Fortune allows,
        I will go live with you there.
        I cannot bear to lose you completely.

FELIPE Father, you leave me no choice 1430
        but to go and do as you say.
        Do not cry.

LAURO   God knows how hard this is for me to say.

        LAURO *starts to leave*

---

21   Fortune's constantly turning wheel was proverbial.

FELIPE   Wait, do not go!

LAURO   This is too difficult.
                We will speak more tonight.
                God keep you,
                and me as well, in my old age,
                so that I may see you again.

                          Exit LAURO

FELIPE   Oh Spain,   1440
                though I live a peaceful life on this mountain,
                I do long to see you,
                especially when I consider
                the great station into which I was born.
                My honor forces me to seek you out,
                to venture my life against all odds.
                Yet if my mother has died at my grandfather's hands
                and Heaven has made my father witness such tyranny
                with no hope of avenging her,
                then what could I do?   1450
                It hardly seems prudent to act recklessly
                and cause yet more misfortune.

                          Enter ROSAURA

ROSAURA   (*Aside*) I have come to see him, that bright sun,
                whatever my mother says.
                Who could blame someone
                who seeks to know more about her own father?
                For although my mother has warned me
                that his light will burn,
                that same fire pleases me
                and the pleasure only grows   1460
                as I watch him leave.
                I cannot live without him.

>   I have lost my appetite,
>   and that is serious!
>   I can't even sleep!
>   I can't understand why my mother
>   would prevent me from seeing
>   the one who my soul so desires.
>   I will find out through experience.
>   She says that if I make my fingers into a cross,   1470
>   demons will flee from me
>   and angels will stay,
>   so I should not be afraid.
>   If he sees the cross
>   and does not leave,
>   then he must be an angel.
>   And if he runs, he is a demon.
>   (*Aloud to* FELIPE) By this cross, be gone!
>   (*Aside*) Oh heavens!
>   He's not moving and remains calm   1480
>   when I make the cross before his eyes.
>   He is an angel, that much is clear.
>   But he may not have seen it...
>   I will call out to him
>   as I make the cross again,
>   just in case.
>   (*Aloud to* FELIPE) Hello, hello!

FELIPE   Who is that?

ROSAURA   Behold the cross!

FELIPE   Holy God preserve me!   1490

ROSAURA   Are you running away?
            So you are a demon.

FELIPE   (*Aside*) But what am I doing?

| | The very flowers will blush
to see such cowardice in me.
I will unsheathe my sword instead.
(*Aloud*) Here I am, fierce monster!
(*Aside*) I am terrified,
but I'll either kill it
or die in the attempt.   1500 |

ROSAURA   Behold the cross!

FELIPE   (*Aloud*) I should say the same to you.
           Why are you saying this to me, you demon?

ROSAURA   (*Aside*) An angel, then, since he stands there.

FELIPE   Who are you, beautiful beast,
           whose face stills my hand and sword?
           Are you a demon or a woman?
           Your rare beauty could be either.

ROSAURA   (*Aside*) At least he speaks like me
           and I can understand him.   1510

FELIPE   (*Aside*) If this is the horrible beast,
           then fear has tricked us all.
           Nature, in all its wisdom,
           would never form a monster of such beauty.

ROSAURA   (*Aside*) I have looked upon the sun
           and my fire has been tempered by his beauty.

FELIPE   (*Aside*) They call this a beast in Hungary?
           They must be the beasts instead!
           (*Aloud*) You are a creature of the sky,
           like a constellation above.   1520
           Your eyes are like stars,

	oh celestial creature.
ROSAURA	(*Aside*) I feel something stir within me,
	now fire, now ice, but so gentle.
	If he were to leave now,
	losing sight of his beauty would kill me.
FELIPE	Let me see your face
	under all that hair.
	I will do you no harm.
	Your face will reveal the truth. 1530
ROSAURA	(*Aloud*) I will, if you too will let yourself be seen.
FELIPE	Are you, by chance, a woman?
ROSAURA	What do you call a creature who loves you?
FELIPE	Woman.
ROSAURA	Then that is what I must be.
FELIPE	So you love me?
ROSAURA	I'm not sure what it is to love.
	Tell me, and if it matches
	what I feel in my breast,
	I will know that it is love. 1540
FELIPE	I suspect that love is like this:[22]
	to look by accident and to be pleased,
	to imprint, through looking, the image on the soul,
	and more so, to imprint one's memory
	even as the soul tries to turn away.

---

22 Felipe and Rosaura exchange love sonnets, drawing on Renaissance theories of love and the poetic tradition.

To find the senses must obey—
no pleasure until they surrender
and give themselves away.
To focus on, for relief and glory,
the subjection of the soul to pain, 1550
and to embrace as sweet tokens of love
each rejection. To lose at each node
all memory, to place one's life
at another's will: this is love.
You know when it is there.

ROSAURA From what you say,
love sounds most remarkable!

FELIPE Those are its cares, its desires, and its fears.

ROSAURA Now I think I know what I feel.

FELIPE Let your heart declare it then. 1560

ROSAURA Hear me out:
I saw, I admired, and from my admiration
was born a pleasure in which I lost myself.
My senses were asleep, all memory
powerless to wake me.
I felt great sorrow, far from my beloved,
and in this absence, found distraction
only imagining myself with the one who
can make me anguish and delight.
A thousand hopes I offer to my pain— 1570
they cheer me, yet on my own, I despair,
and rejoice, and despair again.
I flee from reason and towards pleasure I reach:
this I feel, this I have, this I suffer.
If this is what love entails, I have nothing left to say.

FELIPE	Your portrait of love is not half bad. Your furs hide a silver tongue.
ROSAURA	Who else but love could teach an animal like me?
FELIPE	Where were you born?
ROSAURA	Me? Here. 1580
FELIPE	To whom?
ROSAURA	To another like me.
ROSAURA	Yes, but who fathered you?
ROSAURA	The sun.
FELIPE	The sun?
ROSAURA	That's right, my love.
FELIPE	The sun and a man, you mean.
ROSAURA	What is a 'man'?
FELIPE	I am.
ROSAURA	You? A man? 1590
FELIPE	That's what they call me.
ROSAURA	And now I love you all the more. So my mother could not make me with the sun alone?
FELIPE	No, neither the sun nor she

could make a child without a man like me.

ROSAURA No doubt this makes me doubt...
And if I wanted to make another creature
like me, to keep me company,
will the sun come along with you? 1600

FELIPE If it doesn't rain.

ROSAURA Then we'll wait for a sunny day.

FELIPE (*Aside*) Oh nature so rare,
to bestow such beauty upon this monster.
This one was born, no doubt,
from that older beast,
who must have been overcome
by a natural passion.
(*To* ROSAURA) Tell me,
have you ever seen me before? 1610

ROSAURA I saw you once on a hot afternoon
while you were bathing in a spring.
Heaven itself can attest
that it took all my strength
not to speak to you,
but some mighty power held me back.
What is that which stops a woman?

FELIPE Modesty, which befits any honest lady.

ROSAURA You are driving me wild.

FELIPE Restrain your love for a moment. 1620
You must first figure out
if I love you in return.

ROSAURA	So, when a woman loves a man, he doesn't just feel the same thing?
FELIPE	Sometimes a man might not love her back.
ROSAURA	Why not? Tell me the reason.
FELIPE	He might love another.
ROSAURA	And where can I find this 'Another'?
FELIPE	She will already be in his heart. 1630
ROSAURA	So, you might love Another woman?
FELIPE	I might.
ROSAURA	Rotten luck…
FELIPE	Don't fret, I love you dearly. But tell me: where can I find you?
ROSAURA	I'm right here.
FELIPE	Wait. I hear voices and fear for your life. Stay here and hide. I'll go see who's coming. 1640 But first, tell me your name.
ROSAURA	Rosaura.
FELIPE	Rosaura?
ROSAURA	Yes. Tell me yours.

FELIPE   My name is Felipe.

ROSAURA   Will you come see me again?

FELIPE   How could I not?

ROSAURA   And that Another woman
              that I loathe so much,
              do you love her too?   1650

FELIPE   Dear God, no!
              I burn only for you.

ROSAURA   Then, Felipe, I'll wait right here for you.

FELIPE   We'll see each other soon.

                        Exit FELIPE

ROSAURA   What a beautiful beast a man is!
              I've never seen anyone I liked so much.
              He only just left and already I feel like crying.
              No modesty, whatever that is, can prevent me.
              Let me call out your sweet name, my Felipe,
              how I long for it to echo in these woods!   1660
              Felipe! Hello there, Felipe! By heavens—
              Another must be holding him in her arms...
              This must be what they call jealousy.
              Listen, Another: you'd better let him go at once,
              I'll come and kill you if I suspect
              your beauty is keeping Felipe from me.

Enter SILVANA, *a peasant girl, on the other side of the stage from*
                        ROSAURA

SILVANA	(*Aside*) They've gone.
We were all here picking flowers together,
but the other girls left without waiting for me.
I'll get them back for this.   1670
I'm trembling now...
I pray that this afternoon doesn't turn out as I fear.
They say that the beast has returned to these woods,
and yesterday it knocked out Pascual with a branch.
Belardo had to run into the river
—fully dressed!—
or he'd have paid for his foolishness too.
Fear suddenly seized the girls
who were here with me.
They ran away so quickly,   1680
they dropped more flowers than they'd picked.
I hope I don't run into the beast
on my way back to the village.
ROSAURA	(*Aside*) I can't quite make out
what that is over there,
but it's definitely not a man.
This animal is different,
I can tell by the forehead and the chin.
Felipe's chin was full of hair
and this one doesn't have any there.   1690
Like me, it only grows hair on its head.
It looks a lot like me, in fact.
I must speak to it.
(*To* SILVANA) What are you?
SILVANA	(*Aside*) Oh no!
ROSAURA	No reason to wait,
unless you're waiting to die.
Tell me, right now:
what kind of creature are you?

	Which animal?	1700
SILVANA	(*Aside*) Oh, I'm dead! (*To* ROSAURA) I'm not running away, I'll do whatever you say. I'm not the one who wronged you. I'm another.	
ROSAURA	Another?	
SILVANA	Yes, I swear.	
ROSAURA	(*Aside*) Such luck to run into Another! (*To* SILVANA) So, you're Another?	
SILVANA	I am. (*Aside*) Yet I'm not who she thinks I am. She must take me for another.	1710
ROSAURA	You will be the death of me. You're the reason for all my suffering. Do you know the most beautiful beast in these woods?	
SILVANA	What's its name?	
ROSAURA	Felipe.	
SILVANA	Why yes, I do.	
ROSAURA	(*Aside*) She won't even deny it! She must not have any of that modesty that Felipe was talking about, since she knows him and even talked to him while I held myself back. (*Aloud*) Tell me, despicable Another, who is Felipe?	1720

SILVANA	He's a young man, son of Lauro,
	though he might as well be
	the son of Apollo himself.
	Like Daphne, who was transformed into a laurel,[23]
	he lives a rustic life in a village by these woods. 1730
ROSAURA	Do you love him?
SILVANA	Sure I do.
	My aunt raised him.
ROSAURA	Who is she?
SILVANA	Another woman.
ROSAURA	So are there more Anothers?
SILVANA	Oh yes, the village is full of them.
ROSAURA	(*Aside*) This will be the end of me!
	Oh Felipe, you ingrate!
	You have so many Anothers: 1740
	killing just one of them
	won't make you return to me.
	(*Aloud*) You and Felipe come together, you traitor?
SILVANA	Everyone knows that!
	Oh please, someone help me!
ROSAURA	When do you do that with him?
SILVANA	During the dance, during the celebrations.

---

23   *Apollo*: Greek god of the sun, as well as light, music, poetry, and more. *Daphne*: A nymph whom Apollo loved and pursued against her wishes. To escape his advances, she asked to be turned into a laurel tree.

ROSAURA   What is the dance?

SILVANA   We all make a big circle.

ROSAURA   Show me how.   1750

SILVANA shows ROSAURA *a pair of castanets*

SILVANA   See, I put these on,
          then we all pair up
          and Benito plays for us.

ROSAURA   Show me.

SILVANA demonstrates a dance for ROSAURA

SILVANA   (*Aside*) Oh saints, please blind her.

ROSAURA   Like this?

SILVANA   Christ! Yes, with these in your hands
          you move back and forth.
          (*Aside*) I must get away!

ROSAURA   By Heaven above, Another,   1760
          you won't live to dance another day.

ROSAURA *hits* SILVANA

SILVANA   Ow, she's going to kill me!

ROSAURA   I don't want you to do the dance
          with the one I love.

Enter TEODOSIA

TEODOSIA	What are you doing? Why are you trying to kill this woman?
SILVANA	Woe is me!
ROSAURA	She's not a woman, she's Another!
SILVANA	What wretched luck, the beasts are multiplying! 1770
TEODOSIA	Go, woman.
SILVANA	Heaven save me!

Exit SILVANA, *running away*

ROSAURA	I don't understand all these species like you do. But I know that by letting her run away you're giving Felipe the chance to be with her.
TEODOSIA	Felipe?
ROSAURA	That's the name of the sun you once knew. He told me he was a man, and that he adores, desires, and loves all the Anothers of the village. 1780 That was one of them.
TEODOSIA	(*Aside*) Oh no! (*To* ROSAURA) Have you been talking to someone?
ROSAURA	No, I don't know this 'Someone'. But I talked to Felipe, a most beautiful creature.
TEODOSIA	What Felipe?

ROSAURA   Really?
               He's the one who engendered me with you.

TEODOSIA   You must have talked to a man.   1790

ROSAURA   Yes, mother,
               the one I saw bathing in the spring.
               Let's keep talking about him.
               When he is gone,
               only his name keeps me going.

TEODOSIA   You should have fended him off
               with the sign of the cross…

ROSAURA   No, no, mother of mine.
               I tried over and over again,
               but it was useless.   1800
               He's an angel, not a demon,
               so he didn't run away.
               He stayed put.

TEODOSIA   And you weren't scared of him?

ROSAURA   Aren't you listening?
               I talked to him, he taught me about love,
               and told me what was in his heart.
               He now lives within mine,
               and knows me better than anyone.
               I begged him to be with me,   1810
               and with the sun.

TEODOSIA   And did he?

ROSAURA   No, he went away,
               and my soul went with him.
               He told me he would love me

           as long as Another didn't stop him.
           As luck would have it,
           as soon as he left,
           a creature came along
           and said its name was Another,   1820
           and that it loved Felipe.
           Can you believe the gall?
           I grabbed it by the hair,
           and if you hadn't come along…

TEODOSIA   What have you done, you little fool?

ROSAURA   Oh mother!
           Those beautiful eyes,
           like two sharp thorns,
           have buried themselves deep in my heart.
           You must pull them out at once,   1830
           or by tomorrow you'll find me
           hanging from this great oak.

TEODOSIA   Oh Rosaura,
           you will be my ruin and my downfall!
           Now you know that you are indeed a woman,
           and so you must know this creature is a man.
           Beware, lest he take from you that which
           a noble woman should prize above all things.
           It is a great dishonor to subject yourself
           to a man in this way.   1840

ROSAURA   Well then, mother,
           help me with this thing they call love,
           and tell me how you managed to make me
           without subjecting yourself to this.

TEODOSIA   All in good time.

>   There are some men they call husbands,
>   and I had one of those.
>   It's dishonor and madness
>   to love a man who belongs to another.

ROSAURA   Well, mother,   1850
             can't that man I saw
             be a husband?

TEODOSIA   Yes, when the time comes.
             And then you can be his wife.

ROSAURA   In that case, the time has come.

TEODOSIA   Yes, but it is low and dishonorable
             for an honorable woman
             to display love so openly.
             According to the laws of courtship,
             it is the man who must love.   1860
             For a woman to beg
             is a great disgrace.

ROSAURA   All those laws are wrong.

TEODOSIA   Shush, this is madness.

ROSAURA   Beauty must be pursued
             wherever it is found.
             If a woman cannot live without a husband,
             then she must beg for what she needs.

TEODOSIA   Nature has given men greater perfection,
             and women, greater beauty.   1870
             Each has their role.
             That's just the way it is.

ROSAURA Well, if man is more perfect,
how are women more beautiful?
Is not beauty perfection?

TEODOSIA Someone is coming.
Wait here while I see who it is.
I'll deal with your questions later.

Exit TEODOSIA

ROSAURA No matter what you say,
I will follow my instincts   1880
and love my equal,
make no mistake.
Love is fierce
and can't be tamed by reason.

Enter FELIPE

FELIPE (*Aside*) I think I left her here,
among these flowers.

ROSAURA Felipe!

FELIPE My Rosaura!
I have felt lost in your absence—

ROSAURA And I lost my patience   1890
while you were detained
by your cruel lady, Another.
But I caught her
and had my revenge.

FELIPE It's true that another loves me,
but ever since I saw you, my love,
I've had no thoughts of loving her.

ROSAURA   I just spoke with my mother,
          and she says I am a woman,
          and I can love you honorably,   1900
          as a husband.
          Is that true or did she lie?

FELIPE   Everything she said was true.
          That is the most perfect love
          and gives no offense to Heaven.

ROSAURA   Then show me that you mean it.

FELIPE   Tell me what you want.

ROSAURA   All right, here I go:
          beg me to love you,
          as if you want me to surrender.   1910
          They say this is very important
          for a woman's honor.
          Then I will be your wife
          and you will be my husband.

FELIPE   That's fair.
          Serving, courting, and begging
          are for the man to do.
          And so, I beg you to love me.

ROSAURA   And even if you didn't say it,
          and my good name were ruined,   1920
          I would still surrender to you.
          I am your wife.

FELIPE   And I, your husband.

ROSAURA   But I must ask one thing of you,
          since I am yours now.

FELIPE	Ask me.
ROSAURA	You must not love Another ever again.
FELIPE	You alone will I love
as my very own wife.
But I would also ask 1930
that you not love any others.
ROSAURA	There are 'Others'?
FELIPE	Yes.
ROSAURA	Where?
FELIPE	All over.
ROSAURA	Never mind, I won't love Others.
FELIPE	(*Aside*) Such candor!
I've never heard the like.
[VOICES]	(*Offstage*) There is the dreadful beast!
Quickly! Prepare your weapons! 1940

Enter villagers BELARDO, TIRSO, RISELO, GIL,[24] *and* SILVANA *with various weapons*

BELARDO	You go first, Silvana.
ROSAURA	What is this?
FELIPE	These are the villagers, all up in arms.
Is it you they're searching for?

---

24 Gil's only appearance, with one line below. Could be doubled or substituted for another character.

TIRSO   Come here everyone, I've found it!

FELIPE   Stay back!

GIL   You stay back, by God!

FELIPE   (*To* ROSAURA) Stay behind me.
                  I fear they might kill you.

ROSAURA   Should I climb to a higher place?   1950

FELIPE   Yes, and wait for me there.

              ROSAURA *moves to another part of the stage*

RISELO   Move aside, Felipe!
                  You should not raise your sword against us,
                  defending such a dangerous and evil creature.

FELIPE   It is not right for you to kill her.

TIRSO   What do you mean it's not right?
                  Get out of the way, I say, or by God—

FELIPE   Are you threatening me, you peasant?

SILVANA   While you fought us off,
                  the beast has escaped into the mountains.   1960

RISELO   That was very wrong of you,
                  but it's our fault for showing you
                  more respect than you deserve.
                  Out of our way!
                  We'll chase down that beast.
                  Anyone who defends such a monster
                  is hardly a Christian.

FELIPE	Stop, Riselo! You must know the beast is not an animal, but a woman.	1970
RISELO	Out of the way! If it were a woman, it would not harm another with such fierce cruelty.	
TIRSO	We'll get it, even if you try to stop us.	
FELIPE	Hold, I say, Riselo!	
RISELO	Let me through!	

They fight, and FELIPE *stabs* RISELO

	Oh, you have killed me!	
FELIPE	I tried to warn you!	
BELARDO	You killed Riselo?	1980
SILVANA	He did!	
BELARDO	Get back! Tirso, fire your gun!	
FELIPE	Stay back, peasants!	
TIRSO	There's no staying back now. Turn yourself in or I'll shoot!	
FELIPE	Wait!	
SILVANA	Capture him or kill him!	

TIRSO	Kill him, kill him!	
FELIPE	Friends, I surrender. It was all Riselo's fault.	1990
TIRSO	Hand over your weapon!	
FELIPE	(*Aside*) For the son of a nobleman to surrender to a mob, how shameful!	
TIRSO	Straight to jail with you!	
BELARDO	That's right!	
SILVANA	For my vengeance to lead to this!	
FELIPE	How can this be?	

Exit all VILLAGERS, *taking* FELIPE *prisoner, then* ROSAURA *returns*

ROSAURA	Prisoner, they say?	2000
	No doubt they will kill him now.	
	Where is my strength?	
	Will I allow such a thing?	
	Where is the fierceness	
	these vast woods have given me,	
	the ferocity of my mountain birth?	
	Is this what a love born of such beauty can do?	
	Great oaks, you have seen me tear to pieces	
	animals much stronger than I.	
	Are you not ashamed to see me now,	2010
	calling myself the wife of a man	
	whom they now drag away	
	to suffer and die?	

Clear and crystalline streams,
whose waters I have tinted red
with the blood of wild beasts
from these great mountains:
why do you not reproach me
for allowing those villagers
to bind and take away   2020
that angel for whom you weep?
Take courage, my shrinking heart.
I will follow him and set him free,
or die in the attempt.
I will give him back the freedom
that he gave up to save me.
Hold on, Felipe, I'm on my way.
God forbid you say
that I loved you like a woman,
left you like a coward,   2030
or fled like a beast!

Exit ROSAURA

SCENE 3

Enter TIRSO, BELARDO, SILVANA, *a* MAGISTRATE, *and* LAURO *with* FELIPE, *bound*

MAGISTRATE Make sure the chains are nice and tight!

LAURO See that justice is done, my good men,
but show restraint
if you have any respect for me.

TIRSO You raised a son
—may the devil take him—
who, in order to free a beast,

	killed one of our finest men.	
	What restraint do you expect now?	2040

FELIPE   Father, by my life,
              let them do as they wish.

LAURO   There is no fury
              like that of an angry mob.

SILVANA   Wasn't it sheer malice
              for Felipe to kill poor Riselo?

LAURO   You, Silvana?
              You demand the death of my son,
              whom your own aunt raised?
              If even you speak against him,   2050
              then he is as good as dead,
              and so am I.

SILVANA   Lauro, you know I am right.
              If you consider the facts,
              you must admit that no punishment
              could be too harsh.

FELIPE   Father, are you pleading with these peasants?

MAGISTRATE   See how well he pleads his case!
              I say we send him to the court at once,
              slung across a donkey's back,   2060
              bound in eighty pounds of chains
              with fourteen soldiers to guard him.
              We can't have him here another minute.

LAURO   I have an estate: does that mean nothing to you?
              And what's more, the king will know at once
              who this young man is.

| | He's the best of Castile,
for you must know Felipe is a Spaniard— |
| --- | --- |
| FELIPE | Stop, father, do not reveal such weighty matters.
I would rather they kill me. 2070 |

Enter ROSAURA, *brandishing a club*

| ROSAURA | Daring love has guided me here
to free a noble soul
held captive among barbarians.
Oh husband of mine, never say
that I was cowardly or false,
or that I failed to defend your life,
as you defended mine!
Release Felipe at once! |
| --- | --- |
| TIRSO | Heavens, isn't that the wild beast
that we were hunting in the mountains? 2080 |
| ROSAURA | If anything, I'm her daughter.
Give me my husband, you peasants! |

ROSAURA *attacks the* VILLAGERS

BELARDO	Ow, she's cracked my head open!
MAGISTRATE	Surround her, hold her, restrain her!
Kill her if you must,
or better yet, capture her for the king.
FELIPE	Rosaura, my lady, my love, my wife,
how I wish I could fight by your side!
TIRSO	Get back, everyone.
This gun will make her yield. 2090

FELIPE   Surrender, my love, surrender at once!
                Give yourself up, my Rosaura!

ROSAURA   You want me to die?

FELIPE   Of course not.

ROSAURA   Well then what do you want from me?

FELIPE   I want you to live.

ROSAURA   Will that make you happy?

FELIPE   It will give me my life.

ROSAURA   Then I surrender.

MAGISTRATE   Grab her!   2100

LAURO   Heavens! What's this I'm seeing?

FELIPE   Don't worry, father.

LAURO   Where did you meet this beast?

FELIPE   You will know one day.

MAGISTRATE   What great fortune we've had today!
                The king will bestow great rewards on us.

BELARDO   But this is just the little beast.
                The big one is still out there.

MAGISTRATE   No matter. Peace in this land
                depends upon carting her off to prison,   2110
                as God and the king demand.

TIRSO	Unless the king wants to show her off in his palace.
BELARDO	All of Hungary will come to see her!
MAGISTRATE	We'll send Felipe with her!
BELARDO	Once they get her on the rack she will confess where her mother is soon enough.
LAURO	Felipe, did you have this child with the beast?
FELIPE	My child, sir? How?
LAURO	Oh Heavens! Why afflict me with these troubles in my old age? 2120
ROSAURA	Felipe!
FELIPE	My Rosaura!
ROSAURA	With you, I have no fear of death.
FELIPE	Without you, I have no need for life.

Exit all

End of ACT II

ACT III

SCENE 1

Enter PRIMISLAO, FAUSTINA, FENICIO, *a nobleman*[25] *and other courtiers*

PRIMISLAO   The beast is strangely beautiful.

FAUSTINA   It is a monstrous beauty...

PRIMISLAO   It's rare to come across such a contradiction in nature.

FAUSTINA   Where was it found in the end?

PRIMISLAO   It was caught trying to free a man
it had been consorting with.
Believe it or not, monsters and humans
often make strange bedfellows.   2130

FAUSTINA   It is certainly not the first time, my lord,
and yet it is no less surprising.
There was a dolphin once that fell in love
with a young man who used to swim
and play with it along the coast.

---

25   Fenicio enters for the first time in Act III and only has one speech. Could be doubled with another character.

| | When the young man stopped coming, the dolphin came ashore to look for him, but could never find him and died of sorrow. | 2140 |

PRIMISLAO Ah, yes! Dogs do those things, too,
though that shouldn't surprise us.
When elephants and horses do this,
now those are rare miracles,
like that dolphin of whom you spoke.
This beast seems to love the young villager so much
that it was willing to offer its life to free him.
They say the young man was so grateful,
he killed two men in order to protect it.[26]

FAUSTINA He's not the first to show such gratitude. 2150
Even animals do it, you know.
It is a beastly man who can't show gratitude.

PRIMISLAO Even a lion once showed favor to a slave
who had drawn a thorn from its paw.[27]

FAUSTINA (*Aside*) But I am the true beast…
and so heaven has punished me
by denying me a child.
I betrayed my innocent sister,
and tarnished her chaste honor too.
I did it for love… 2160
Yet that is no excuse.
Oh inhuman betrayal!
Procne killed her own son
to avenge her sister Philomela,

---

26 Felipe only killed one person, but his crimes seem to have been exaggerated by hearsay.

27 Reference to Androcles, a Christian pardoned by Roman emperor Tiberius after a lion, which recognized him as the person who had pulled a thorn from his paw, refused to attack him.

     whom the king, her husband, had violated.[28]
     How, then, can I go on
     when I took my own sister's life
     after she showed me only kindness?

PRIMISLAO (*To* FAUSTINA) What are you mumbling about, my dear?

FAUSTINA (*Aloud*) About the power of love.   2170
     Even this beast would risk its own life for it.
     Never mind, where shall we display it?

PRIMISLAO Had it been a horrid creature,
     I'd have locked it away in a cage.
     But since it is so lovely,
     we should tie it up in the palace gallery,
     at least during the day,
     so it can enjoy some light and air.

FAUSTINA But the very people who would come to see it
     might also harm it.   2180
     I don't even think it's an animal:
     it speaks, it thinks, it feels.
     It will surely die of frustration.

PRIMISLAO I will assign a guard
     to protect it from the crowd,
     and make sure it doesn't harm anyone.

FAUSTINA What an excellent idea,
     someone who can keep it safe.

FENICIO Among those who flocked to see the beast,

---

  28 *Procne, Philomela*: Two sisters in Greek mythology whose story begins similarly to Teodosia and Faustina (a queen is homesick and asks for her sister to come keep her company), but ends with rape, filicide, and cannibalism.

	there's one villager who they say knew it	2190

there's one villager who they say knew it 2190
and was beloved by it in turn.
They say he often shared fruit and bread with it.

PRIMISLAO If there's a villager who knows the beast
and can speak with it,
then he will make the best guard.
Go and call him right away!

Exit FENICIO, *then enter a* SERVANT

SERVANT The count of Barcelona's ambassador is here.

PRIMISLAO Send him in.

Exit SERVANT, *then enter the* AMBASSADOR, *carrying a letter*

AMBASSADOR I kiss your feet, your majesty.

PRIMISLAO Give me your arms instead. 2200
I welcome you as my equal.
You may sit here by me, Spaniard.

AMBASSADOR Any of your envoys to the count of Barcelona
would receive the same honors.

PRIMISLAO, FAUSTINA *and the* AMBASSADOR *sit down*

PRIMISLAO How is the count?

AMBASSADOR He is full of grief and sorrow.
This letter which I bring to you now
explains the reason.

PRIMISLAO Proceed.

AMBASSADOR The former count 2210
            —may he rest in peace—
            raised his nephew,
            son of the king of Aragon and Naples,
            in his own palace.
            The boy grew up with the count's beautiful daughter.
            Equals in beauty, age, and position,
            they even shared the same blood,
            and seemed fated to fall in love.
            They married in secret,
            though no love can be kept secret for long. 2220
            The count eventually found out
            and discovered they had a lovely son,
            who was being raised secretly in the palace.
            Though he did not know who the boy was,
            the count came to love him so dearly
            that he would not even eat if the boy was not there.

PRIMISLAO   Was it his own blood calling to him?

AMBASSADOR No, not at all,
            or else he would have restrained his cruel fury
            when he found out who the child was. 2230
            Instead, he imprisoned his nephew,
            who was now his son-in-law,
            locked his daughter in a convent,
            and condemned the child to death—
            though he did not want it to be a violent one.
            He sent three noblemen away with the child
            with orders to leave him somewhere.
            On an island, on a mountain, in the woods—
            it didn't matter, as long as it was far away from Spain.
            And that's what they did. 2240
            For as long as he lived,
            the count would never budge.
            Neither the tears of his wife,

nor the letters from the Pope,
nor the threat of war from Aragón,
nor the pleas of Castile and France
could persuade him to pardon his nephew.
When the count finally died,
his nephew claimed the throne
by securing the church's consent 2250
to officially marry his cousin.[29]
Now, the new count has fallen ill
and the countess rules in his stead,
though many are rebelling.[30]
Their son must be found immediately.
One of the three noblemen who abandoned the boy,
though now frail and ancient,
has information that can help.
He claims he left Felipe here in Hungary,
on a barren mountain that looks out to Spain, 2260
battered by the sea.
If Felipe is still alive in some city or town,
he must be about 29 or 30 by now.
That's why I'm here, my lord.
The count asks that you take pity
on our land and on the countess by requesting that
Felipe be sought across your kingdom.
The desolate countess begs the same of you
in this letter, my lady. (*Gives the letter to* FAUSTINA)

PRIMISLAO   It pains me to learn of this sad case. 2270
I had heard something of it.
I am heartened to think that Felipe might be alive,
and here in Hungary no less.
May fortune smile upon us
and may you find your lord.

---

29   First cousins needed a special dispensation from the Pope in order to marry.
30   See Introduction for more discussion of female rulers in history and fiction.

AMBASSADOR Thank you, your majesty.
　　　　　　　Your good will towards our afflicted land
　　　　　　　revives our lost hopes.

FAUSTINA　　Let me offer you some advice,
　　　　　　　call it woman's intuition, if you will: 　　　　2280
　　　　　　　don't tell anyone who you're looking for,
　　　　　　　lest you be deceived with false signs.
　　　　　　　Who wouldn't risk it all
　　　　　　　for the sake of a throne?

PRIMISLAO　 What good advice!
　　　　　　　I will provide you with some men
　　　　　　　who will help you discreetly.

FAUSTINA　　(*Aside*) I spoke from the heart.
　　　　　　　My own deception taught me that lesson.

AMBASSADOR I am at your feet, your majesty. 　　　　　2290

PRIMISLAO　 I will send out some secret letters on your behalf.
　　　　　　　Officers and noblemen across the kingdom
　　　　　　　will diligently undertake the search,
　　　　　　　just to earn my favor.
　　　　　　　Meanwhile, you may rest here, Spaniard.
　　　　　　　May the heavens grant you a favorable resolution
　　　　　　　after all these years.

AMBASSADOR May God bless you and keep you.

　　　　　　　Exit the AMBASSADOR

PRIMISLAO　 What a strange tale, Faustina.

FAUSTINA　　It brings back sad memories. 　　　　　　　　2300

| PRIMISLAO | I am heartened by the thought
that our own dear, lost child
could also be alive in the woods. |
|---|---|
| FAUSTINA | Alas, this stirs up memories of that fateful day,
when the frightful beast snatched from my arms
my innocent babe, now surely an angel in Heaven.
They brought me a dead infant
and claimed it was mine,
but now I fear that it was a ploy
by some cunning peasant, my lord,   2310
who was merely seeking a reward.
I had not thought of this in years,
but hearing of another's misfortune
has reawakened my sorrows.
Now I must seek out this beast
and find some answers at last. |
| PRIMISLAO | Oh, my love!
These thoughts only renew our suffering. |

Enter FABIO, *a page*[31]

| FABIO | Here comes the peasant
who claims he can calm the beast.   2320 |
|---|---|

Exit FABIO, *then enter* TEODOSIA, *disguised as a rustic peasant*

TEODOSIA	I am at your feet, your majesty.
FAUSTINA	Speak, my good man.
TEODOSIA	(*Aside*) "My good sister" she could say,
had she been less cruel to me.

---

[31]   Fabio's only line and appearance. Could be doubled or substituted for another character (possibly Fenicio).

FAUSTINA   Is the beast human? Does it reason?
            Where did you first encounter and befriend it?
            How did you come to love such a hideous creature?
            Did it tell you that its mother was another beast,
            the cause of all my misfortune?

TEODOSIA   I wouldn't want to speak out of turn, 2330
            and peasants shouldn't opine about what royals do,
            just look on in silence and reverence.
            Yet they say that no sooner had Teodosia,
            the queen of Hungary—your sister, I believe—
            died due to false suspicions,
            then a beast suddenly appeared in the woods
            unlike anything ever seen before.
            There are those who say, my lady,
            that it was the soul of the queen
            come to take her revenge. 2340
            But those are merely superstitions,
            which good Christians must discount.
            What is more, this beast had an appetite.
            It stole bread, milk, cattle,
            wine, cheese and nuts,
            and everyone knows that souls don't eat.
            Once there is no body,
            no bodily needs remain.
            It lived there for some years, as you know,
            until the day you went hunting 2350
            by the banks of that fateful stream.
            There, on the green grass,
            you gave birth to a beautiful daughter
            whom the beast stole.
            Are you crying?

FAUSTINA   How could I not weep at such a terrible tragedy?

TEODOSIA   Should I stop?

FAUSTINA	No, keep going.
TEODOSIA	A shepherd who dabbled in magic
and used the stars to tell men's fortunes   2360
claimed that Heaven created this rare beast
precisely for the purpose of stealing that babe.
For some years, our villages had nothing to fear.
Then suddenly, two beasts appeared in the woods:
a big one and the smaller one you have here.
They say there's a whole lineage of them
that inhabit these mountains.
One day, it stole my daughter from our cottage,
and I gave chase, spurred by a father's love.
I followed it up to the highest peaks,   2370
and when I finally caught up to it,
I fell on my knees and begged the beast
to feed on me instead of her.
It took pity on us and I offered it
two goats, ten sheep, three fine woolen blankets,
and four or five pieces of cloth as ransom.
Since that day, my lady, it grew so fond of me
that I learned its language from our conversations.
I asked what they did with those young children
they snatched from their parents   2380
and it told me—perish the thought!—
that they sacrificed them to their great idol.
Would you like me to ask about yours,
to see if it is dead or alive?
Then we'll know for sure if it is alive or dead.
PRIMISLAO	Cease this tale of woe.
TEODOSIA	If I have caused offense,
I beg your forgiveness.
PRIMISLAO	Teodosia was put to death for good reason.

| | Let the rabble believe what they may.   2390
              I am satisfied that justice was done. |

| TEODOSIA | You're right, never mind the rabble—
             they despise today what they'll praise tomorrow.
             They are as fickle as Fortune itself,
             and would rule over kings if they could.
             They hold all authority in contempt
             and respect no one.
             They only speak kindly of Teodosia
             because you married her sister
             so soon thereafter.   2400 |

| PRIMISLAO | I know how the rabble is. |

| TEODOSIA | But you and Faustina,
             your consciences are clean, I'm sure. |

| FAUSTINA | How rude! That's enough!
             (*To* PRIMISLAO) Don't listen to him! |

| TEODOSIA | I say this only because I know
             you received a dispensation to marry each other.
             I pray Heaven grants you many children to succeed
                                                                    you. |

| FAUSTINA | Teodosia was a traitor to the king,
             to Heaven, and to this land.   2410
             I was the one who revealed all this to the king,
             and so I deserve his love, esteem, and adoration. |

| TEODOSIA | No doubt. |

| FAUSTINA | My good man, you well know that on that day
             the beast robbed me of my greatest treasure.
             Find out whether the child was sacrificed |

	in those hideous rites, or if she still lives.	
TEODOSIA	Leave it all to me.	
PRIMISLAO	Will you understand what it says?	
TEODOSIA	I will.	2420
PRIMISLAO	Then you must take charge of this beast as its keeper and guard— with appropriate compensation, of course.	
TEODOSIA	May heaven grant you a long life and increase your line.	
[VOICES]	(*Offstage*) Watch out for the monster!	
FAUSTINA	It's coming.	
TEODOSIA	What are you afraid of?	
FAUSTINA	It reminds me of that other beast who took everything from me.	2430
[VOICES]	(*Offstage*) Watch out for the monster!	
FAUSTINA	Oh beast, how can I look upon that face of yours, so similar to that cruel one which caused all my sorrows?	

Enter some pages, CELIO *and* LIDIO, *running from* ROSAURA

CELIO	Lidio, watch out for the beast!
LIDIO	Heaven help me!

ROSAURA   If you harm me, shall I not defend myself?

TEODOSIA   Stop!

ROSAURA *and* TEODOSIA *whisper to each other*

ROSAURA   Mother!   2440
Tell me who all these people are.

TEODOSIA   Didn't I tell you not to call me that here?

ROSAURA   Tell me, who is that man?

TEODOSIA   He who gave you life.

ROSAURA   What do you mean?

TEODOSIA   That's the king.

ROSAURA   What is 'King'?

TEODOSIA   He who rules over others.

PRIMISLAO   (*Aside*) She's so fearsome…

ROSAURA *and* TEODOSIA *continue to whisper to each other*

TEODOSIA   He makes the laws;   2450
he depends on no other;
he represents God on earth.

ROSAURA   So why aren't you the king,
since you do all that?

TEODOSIA   I did rule once,
but human malice got in the way.

ROSAURA	Didn't you appeal to divine justice?
TEODOSIA	I called out to God through my suffering.
ROSAURA	I will tear them to pieces. And that one? 2460
TEODOSIA	The queen.
ROSAURA	What is 'Queen'?
TEODOSIA	The king's wife.
ROSAURA	Does she also make laws?
TEODOSIA	No, Rosaura.
ROSAURA	Well then, what does she do? What is she for?
TEODOSIA	She makes more kings so they can make more laws. From this queen another king is born, 2470 and from that one, yet another, and that's how their power endures.
ROSAURA	Hmm, I might like to be a queen.
TEODOSIA	A more fortunate one than I, I hope.
ROSAURA	It seems like a nice job, to make kings. I will ask the king if he will decree that thirty or forty be birthed from me, if it's for the common good.

TEODOSIA	Watch out, the queen is listening to you
and will soon grow jealous.   2480
She who would gladly kill her own sister to rule,
wouldn't hesitate to kill her own daughter.
ROSAURA	What, whose daughter am I?
TEODOSIA	A false queen's.

Enter the ADMIRAL *of Hungary*

CELIO	The admiral is here!
TEODOSIA	(*Aside to* ROSAURA) Hush now.
Do as I do.
ADMIRAL	May the heavens keep you safe.
PRIMISLAO	Well, Admiral, what's the news from England?
ADMIRAL	Their king is taking up arms against your land 2490
because of a false rumor.
FAUSTINA	My father is attacking us?
ADMIRAL	This rumor dishonors you,
claiming that you killed the thing
he cherished most in the world.
They say that to become queen of Hungary...
FAUSTINA	Stop, say no more.
ADMIRAL	I didn't mean to offend you.
PRIMISLAO	If your words displease the queen,
hold your tongue.   2500

ADMIRAL   They are saying that Teodosia was a saint.

TEODOSIA   (*Aside*) I have certainly suffered enough.

ADMIRAL   In Scotland, too, people are taking up arms to help,
           because their prince complains
           that she was unjustly accused of loving him.

PRIMISLAO That's enough, Admiral.
           Put an end to your tales.
           You must look to our defense now
           and stop talking about the past.

ADMIRAL   We should take every precaution.   2510
           Their armies are advancing, under royal command.

PRIMISLAO Survey our forces in the garrisons
           and those who can guard the coast.
           I will put an end to this false rumor,
           and show that Teodosia's death was well-deserved.

ADMIRAL   Yes, your majesty.

The ADMIRAL *exits;* ROSAURA *and* TEODOSIA *resume whispering to each other*

ROSAURA   Who was that?

TEODOSIA   The admiral.

ROSAURA   What is 'Admiral'?

TEODOSIA   A high-ranking officer.   2520
           He is like a general on the sea, leading the ships.
           His flagship flies the royal banner on behalf of the king.

ROSAURA I've seen ships before,
and you told me what they were for.
But who is that other king they speak of,
and why is he waging war?

TEODOSIA He rules another kingdom.
He is father to the queen and Teodosia,
the one I told you was wrongfully killed,
if you recall. 2530

ROSAURA The queen is the one who deserves to die,
from what I've seen.

Enter a MAGISTRATE *with a paper, pen and ink*

LIDIO The magistrate is here.

PRIMISLAO (*To the* MAGISTRATE) What is it you want?

MAGISTRATE I have a death sentence for you to sign.

PRIMISLAO Show me.

MAGISTRATE I assume you already know what happened.

PRIMISLAO What?

MAGISTRATE It concerns the youth who murdered a man
to free this monster. 2540

PRIMISLAO He is sentenced to death?

MAGISTRATE He does not deny his crime,
and it is an atrocious one.

PRIMISLAO   Show me the order.

MAGISTRATE Here it is, in writing.

ROSAURA   (*Aloud*) Heavens, will you allow this?
            Eyes, will you witness this?
            Arms, will you endure this?
            Oh King, what are you signing?
            Do you know what you are doing?   2550
            Don't be so hasty.
            You'll be damned if you do
            —or rather, I will.
            A God-given life should not be taken so lightly.
            You can give gold and honor
            to those whom you want to ennoble,
            but you can't give them life.
            The very idea is nonsense.
            So, don't be so quick to take away
            that which you cannot give.   2560

PRIMISLAO   I will excuse this disrespect,
            coming from a monster like you.
            But if you know so much,
            you must also know that if a crime is committed,
            God allows death as a punishment
            for those who are guilty.
            I sign because it is just.
            A king, in imitation of God,
            bestows both rewards and punishments.

ROSAURA   I don't know about the law,   2570
            but I say this is an unjust verdict.
            Following my natural reason,
            I think the one who first caused all this trouble
            deserves the punishment.

MAGISTRATE	The law agrees: how could it be otherwise?
	The one who first caused the harm
	is the one at fault.
ROSAURA	If that is the case,
	is it not a clear injustice
	to pierce Felipe's innocent breast? 2580
	Since I am the one who caused this,
	I should be put to death.
	Long live that man,
	death to this monster!
FAUSTINA	(*Aside*) I am shaken to my core.
TEODOSIA	(*Aside*) What can I do, wretch that I am?
	I can't reveal her identity amid all this confusion.
PRIMISLAO	Prepare the prisoner for his execution.
ROSAURA	(*Aside*) I must not be afraid!
PRIMISLAO	Seize the beast and throw it in prison! 2590
ROSAURA	(*Aloud*) You'll never catch me!
PRIMISLAO	Stop, beast!
MAGISTRATE	I will execute the sentence.

The MAGISTRATE *exits*

ROSAURA	What do you mean, "execute"?
	Not so fast, traitors,
	you will kill him over my dead body.

FAUSTINA	(*To* PRIMISLAO) I feel an inexplicable pity, an odd tenderness for the beast.
PRIMISLAO	(*To* FAUSTINA) I feel it too.

Exit FAUSTINA *and* PRIMISLAO

TEODOSIA	(*Aside*) How can I stand by and watch this? (*Aloud*) Stop, Rosaura, by God!	2600
ROSAURA	(*To* CELIO) What's this? Do you think you can catch me?	
CELIO	Lidio, give me a hand over here!	
LIDIO	Who, me?	
TEODOSIA	(*Aside*) She is blinded by love!	
CELIO	(*To* LIDIO) Let's try it together.	
LIDIO	Where is it going?	
TEODOSIA	(*Aloud*) Wait!	
ROSAURA	I must free my love.	2610
CELIO	Guards!	
ROSAURA	Get out of my way!	
CELIO	Sound the alarm! The beast runs free!	

Exit all

SCENE 2

Enter FELIPE, *in chains, with* LAURO

LAURO   My son, you must seek a way out of this prison.

FELIPE   Dear father, I am sorry to cause you such grief.
I suffer when I see you suffer.
But if you intend to reveal who I am,
this is not the right time,
given the danger from my homeland.   2620
If the one who wished me dead
learns that I'm still alive,
if that tyrant—for so I must call my grandfather—
or one of his people find out,
he will try once again to kill me
to prevent me from claiming what is mine.

LAURO   I am moved by your plight, Felipe,
and fear the danger that may come to pass—
one who loves always fears the worst.
Misfortune comes quick, good fortune hangs back,   2630
and we fool ourselves if we think otherwise.

FELIPE   What will they do with me?

LAURO   I can't imagine they will seek
anything less than your execution.
You must let me clear this up.
A low peasant cannot demand your death.

Enter NOTARY *and* WARDEN

WARDEN   That's him over there.

NOTARY	Are you Felipe, from the Prado de Miraflor?[32]
FELIPE	I am.
NOTARY	Then I must inform you 2640 that you have been condemned to death.
LAURO	To death?
FELIPE	I appeal this and beg mercy of the king.
NOTARY	The king himself has signed this decree, so there is nothing to appeal, and no one to appeal to.
FELIPE	Then I have nothing else to say.
LAURO	Why not? I will go to the king myself— this terrible decree must not be carried out.
FELIPE	Oh father, father… 2650
WARDEN	This old man is your father?
FELIPE	Yes, sir.
WARDEN	I'm so sorry!
NOTARY	What an ill fate.
[VOICES]	(*Offstage*) Beware the wild animal! Beware the beast! Beware, it's in the prison now!

---

32   Presumably the name of Felipe and Lauro's home village.

NOTARY	What is that?	
WARDEN	The monster has escaped from the palace, and come to the prison.	2660
NOTARY	How strange!	
WARDEN	This is unheard of!	

Enter ROSAURA *with a club*

ROSAURA	Get out of my way, villains!	
NOTARY	Gladly!	
WARDEN	Let's tie it up by its hands and feet!	
NOTARY	Easier said than done.	
WARDEN	Is that so? Then I'll go get a musket.	

Exit the WARDEN *and* NOTARY

ROSAURA	(*To* FELIPE) Am I dreaming, my love? Can it be that fortune grants my desire to lay eyes upon you again?	2670
FELIPE	My love, can it really be you, in the flesh, whom I now see with my very own eyes?	
ROSAURA	Oh Felipe, how long were the hours spent away from you!	
FELIPE	Oh Rosaura, how painful was your absence from my side!	

ROSAURA   How have you fared in this dark prison, my beloved?

FELIPE   How could I fare without you?
           That was my real misfortune.   2680
           How did you fare out there,
           in the royal palace, without me?

ROSAURA   Without you, I become an animal again.

FELIPE   You, an animal,
           when the light of your eyes
           calms my restless heart?

ROSAURA   What else would you call
           one who lives without her soul?
           For when I am away from you, Felipe,
           I am without my soul.   2690
           If they call me an animal then,
           they are right, for my soul is absent.

FELIPE   Oh Rosaura,
           I have some distressing news—
           they have sentenced me to death.

ROSAURA   I know, my darling.
           That is why I am distraught.
           But don't be afraid.

FELIPE   Since I fell in love with you, Rosaura,
           I have learned the meaning of fear.   2700
           What did you see in the palace?
           Tell me all about it.

ROSAURA   I saw lives rushing apace.
           I saw kings, supreme officers of justice and government.
           I saw a second Flood and burning flames.

> I saw the Judgement Day:
> a torrent of ambitious men,
> reaching and grasping as they pass,
> an inferno of those aspiring to great office,
> again and again and again. 2710
> The whole world gathered there,
> all of humanity on parade.
> I saw so many gaudy riches
> doing no one any good.
> I saw the beauty the countryside freely displays
> rendered with great artifice.
> I saw how powerful flattery can be,
> and enough pomp and circumstance to fill a book.
> I saw the power of the crown,
> and a staircase of glass 2720
> on which some rose,
> and some came crashing down.
> I saw the great titles and offices that everyone vies for,
> though their pursuit seems long
> when life is so short.
> I saw men wittier than they were wise,
> while those who spoke of science and truth
> were kept at the door.
> In short, with much sorrow,
> I looked upon that whole elegant machine, 2730
> and said to myself:
> "How fine this would all be
> if death did not await us all."

FELIPE No one who heard you speak, my love,
would call you an animal.
Natural intelligence clearly reveals a divine soul
to any who can see.

ROSAURA I must get you out of here right now.

FELIPE	The king will let me out, but only to die.	2740

ROSAURA   Not as long as I live.

Enter the WARDEN *and a* SERVANT *with a musket and chains*

WARDEN   Don't shoot!

SERVANT   Why not?
It's sure to fight back.

WARDEN   Surrender yourself, you savage!

ROSAURA	You fool! How could I do that when Felipe is still in his cell? You have no idea how I love him. The whole world could not stop me if I chose to defend myself. But no, I will not resist: I will remain by Felipe's side. Come then, and put me in chains. If my story is to end today, I seek no greater glory than to share his pain.	2750

SERVANT   Such words from a beast!

ROSAURA   Go on, hurry up.
Love is the only prison I need.

The SERVANT *chains* ROSAURA

SERVANT	I have chained the beast. It has the most beautiful face…	2760

WARDEN	Stay there while the king decides what to do with you.
FELIPE	My love, I am crushed to see these chains upon you.
ROSAURA	A thousand deaths with you
would only give me pleasure.
FELIPE	That would be the greatest glory.
There can be no misfortune amid such joy.

Exit all

SCENE 3

Enter TEODOSIA

TEODOSIA   I tread with mortal fear through this palace
where I was once esteemed,
and find myself asking the heavens   2770
what they have in store for me.
The king is haughty towards my sister,
and she trembles with guilt.
The servants whisper of my innocence,
and the heavens reward me for my patience.
My father is approaching with his army,
and the king sues for peace.
The prince of Scotland will not be appeased
and demands my conniving sister's death.
The winds of change will topple this house of cards.   2780
Meanwhile, in my disguise I watch and wait.
Here comes Faustina with the admiral.
I will hide here.

TEODOSIA *hides as* FAUSTINA *and the* ADMIRAL *enter*

FAUSTINA	Wait, hear me out.
ADMIRAL	Don't be too hasty. You'll only make things worse.
FAUSTINA	You know I made you who you are. Though you were but a poor gentleman, I granted you this office in return for your help. Together we forged those love letters 2790 from the prince of Scotland that destroyed my innocent sister. My father stayed silent for so long because he believed in Teodosia's guilt. Now moved by the heavens, or by the force of truth itself, he claims that I was the one at fault. He is on his way to punish me and restore Teodosia's honor. And with my father approaching, 2800 my husband no longer looks kindly upon me.
ADMIRAL	Well then, how will you deal with him?
FAUSTINA	I will poison him and put an end to all of this, crowning you king instead, so you can shield me from my father's fury.
ADMIRAL	These promises of glory and this high rank you offer outdo all prior loyalty and obligations. But look out, here comes the king.
FAUSTINA	Have no fear: I will take care of him. 2810 I will scatter some poisoned rose petals plucked from my hair into his drink— a trick I learned from the beautiful Cleopatra

	in the wine she offered Mark Antony.[33]
ADMIRAL	We are not safe here.
FAUSTINA	Then come with me. Let's discuss this in the gardens.

Exit FAUSTINA *and the* ADMIRAL

TEODOSIA	What a stroke of luck! I have always mistrusted that admiral! Now Heaven has allowed me to learn of their plot. 2820

Exit TEODOSIA

SCENE 4

Enter PRIMISLAO, *the* AMBASSADOR *of Barcelona,*
LAURO, CELIO *and* LIDIO

LAURO	I'm only telling you this now because you've sentenced Felipe to death.
PRIMISLAO	It is such a strange story!
AMBASSADOR	Send for him, sir.
LAURO	Ambassador, are you the one searching for my beloved prisoner?
AMBASSADOR	Indeed, I have come from Spain to find him, and if he is Felipe,

---

33 Cleopatra was known to experiment with poisons. This story is found in Pliny's *Natural History* (Book XXI.9).

	you will be richly rewarded.
LAURO	I have kept both the clothes and the jewels 2830
he was wearing when I first found him.
And see these—my white hairs.
My last day is upon me.
There would be nothing for me to gain
in deceiving the king now.
PRIMISLAO	(*To* LIDIO) Go and fetch Felipe!
AMBASSADOR	It must be him.
LAURO	Indeed it is.
CELIO	Be careful,
the beast is in the cell with him. 2840
PRIMISLAO	But why?
CELIO	It heard of his impending death
and went to set him free.
PRIMISLAO	Incredible!
Bring them both here!

Exit LIDIO

| LAURO | One afternoon, in my fiery youth,
I was hunting at the foot of that great mountain
that rises near the sea,
when I heard the piteous cries of young Felipe, your lord.
I went to him and helped him down from the rock. 2850
He told me who he was,
and who had left him there with no means of escape. |

	The names of those men were Fulgencio and Arfindo.[34]
AMBASSADOR	Those were indeed their names, good man.
	What more proof do we need?
	Lauro, your prayers have been answered.
	Felipe will find favor once more.

Enter FELIPE, ROSAURA, LIDIO, *and other servants*

FELIPE	...And you shall be a queen too.
ROSAURA	How sad you're making me![35]
AMBASSADOR	There is no need to tell me who this young man is: 2860
	he is the spitting image of the count.
	Oh, how cruel the years have been!
	My lord, I weep at your feet and beg for your hands.
FELIPE	And who are you?
AMBASSADOR	Your noble parents' ambassador.
PRIMISLAO	He is of such royal countenance
	that I must believe it.
	(*To* FELIPE) Let me embrace you.
FELIPE	I can't make sense of this sudden fortune.
	Let me kiss your hands, my lord. 2870
PRIMISLAO	Come here, Felipe.
ROSAURA	(*Aside*) So he's a count and a nobleman?
	What will become of me?

---

34 Plácido has been left out, perhaps forgotten by Lauro (or the author).

35 Rosaura is worried that Felipe's new position will take him away from her and their love.

PRIMISLAO	Come, Felipe, you and the ambassador must dine with me.
FELIPE	We shall do as you wish and accept this great honor.
ROSAURA	Hey, King!
PRIMISLAO	What do you want, savage beast?
ROSAURA	To eat with him. 2880
PRIMISLAO	(*Aside*) It's getting worked up again.
ROSAURA	Felipe, don't go and leave me here by myself.
FELIPE	Be quiet and wait here.
ROSAURA	I see. You command me like a lord. Well, you ingrate, upon my life, I will snatch away the table and the feast and throw it all out the window, and you both along with it!
PRIMISLAO	Tie the monster to this column! But not too tight, don't hurt it. 2890
ROSAURA	What is 'tie'?
CELIO	Just let me do it!

Exit PRIMISLAO, *the* AMBASSADOR, FELIPE, *and* LAURO

ROSAURA	You fiends, I'll break this chain and all of you into a thousand pieces so you can never do this to anyone else.

Enter TEODOSIA

TEODOSIA   Stop fighting, Rosaura.
           If Felipe is who they say he is,
           you shall be his wife.

ROSAURA   What do you mean?

TEODOSIA   A queen would make a fitting wife for him.   2900

ROSAURA   What do you mean, a queen?

TEODOSIA   Let them tie you up.

ROSAURA   For your sake, mother, I will submit.

LIDIO   (*Aside*) Who cares whether it is out of fear or respect,
           we've got it now.

CELIO *and* LIDIO *tie* ROSAURA *to a column with a long chain*

TEODOSIA   Wait here, Rosaura,
           while I sort things out.

Exit TEODOSIA

ROSAURA   How can you leave me here in such a state?
           Oh soul hidden beneath this rough exterior,
           are you capable of feeling?   2910
           Then my soul says: "Can you not see that I am?"
           And of understanding?
           "In understanding I am naturally blessed."
           And of acting with free will?
           "Do you not see it in the one I choose to love,
           despite the suffering it brings?"
           And what of memory?

"That too, and at any moment,
I am ready to fly on its wings."
Well then, my soul, 2920
if you love, understand, and remember,
and your love is led by your understanding and memory,
then do not lose your mind,
but hold onto those faculties that God has given you
to distinguish good from bad,
punishment from glory.[36]

Enter PABLOS,[37] *a jester, and two or three pages with a plate of sweets*

CELIO	(*To* PABLOS) Those are not for you, you monster. They are for the other animal.
PABLOS	Can't I have them, since I was born so beastly? Give them to me or else. 2930
LIDIO	Don't give them to him. We need those treats to tame the beast. Oh beast, would you like one of these?
PABLOS	(*To* ROSAURA) Say no and tell them to give them all to me. I swear I saw when they were cooking them, and they left out the sugar. Also, they will ruin your teeth.
CELIO	I think it doesn't like you.
PABLOS	Then I will hit it with this stool. 2940

---

36 Rosaura here outlines the faculties that differentiate a human from an animal. For more, see the introduction.

37 Pablos enters for the first time in Act III. Could be doubled with another character.

ROSAURA	If only I could move!
CELIO	Take them, take them, and don't hurt us.
PABLOS	Do not eat them, you animal, or I will strike you!
ROSAURA	You fiends! If only I were not tied up…
PABLOS	Free yourself then, or let the devil take you!
ROSAURA	How dare you touch me when I am wild to the core!
PABLOS	Untie yourself then, and let's go three rounds for the first bite. 2950
ROSAURA	I do not eat things brought to me by my mortal enemy.
PABLOS	What do you eat then?
ROSAURA	Hands and feet!
PABLOS	Good God! And stomachs too. It seems that we have similar tastes in food.
LIDIO	(*Aside to* CELIO) Go shove him from behind.
CELIO	(*Aside to* LIDIO) Watch me.

CELIO *and* LIDIO *push* PABLOS *and he falls down where* ROSAURA *grabs him*

PABLOS	Oh! Oh!

CELIO   That was a good one!   2960

ROSAURA   Now you'll pay!

  While ROSAURA *is beating* PABLOS, TEODOSIA *enters*

TEODOSIA   Stop, Rosaura, this is not the time.

PABLOS   It's killing me!

TEODOSIA   Flee, villain, while you still can.

PABLOS   Maybe it's drunk, too!

  Exit CELIO, LIDIO, *and* PABLOS

ROSAURA   What else should I do, mother?

TEODOSIA   Listen: the king and his court are in an uproar.
               While at dinner the king was given a letter
               claiming Faustina, whom they call the queen,
               planned to slip him poison in his wine.   2970
               They're testing it now to see if it's true
               that the flowers from her hair would have killed him.

ROSAURA   But how does her crime remedy my misfortune?

TEODOSIA   Wait, listen! Do you hear those drums?
               The king of England approaches.
               Rosaura, your happiness now begins.

ROSAURA   What do I care for drums and wine,
               if I am without Felipe?

  Enter the king of ENGLAND, *the prince of* SCOTLAND, *and
  soldiers*

ENGLAND   You can't stop me!

SCOTLAND   Reserve your fury, sire,   2980
until you know who is to blame.

ENGLAND   If it turns out to be Primislao,
I will not leave a single battlement standing in all his lands.

Enter PRIMISLAO, FAUSTINA, FELIPE, *the* AMBASSADOR, LAURO, *and others*

PRIMISLAO   Sir, what manner of visit is this?
Have I not offered you safe passage through my lands?
Have I ever kept you from either my cities or my armies?
Have I not raised my banners for you
on every ship and castle,
on land and at sea?

ENGLAND   My quarrel is not with you,   2990
but with that ingrate daughter of mine.

PRIMISLAO   Such an ingrate that you will wish she were not yours.
You are here just in time, sir, to learn
how she matches the Greeks and the Romans in malice,
with their treasons and countless evil deeds.
I was just at dinner with Felipe,
son of the beautiful countess of Barcelona,
who was raised since boyhood in a village near here.
At the table, I learned that Faustina,
that ungrateful beast,   3000
wished to poison me
and marry the grand admiral of Hungary.
I immediately tested her poison
and discovered the whole truth.

ENGLAND   A swift remedy to your misfortunes!

| | But what of my own?
Faustina, you traitor!
How could you destroy the holiness,
the innocence of that sweet angel, Teodosia?
Don't answer and offer me a response   3010
that would cost you your life!

FELIPE   My lord, bear this blow from blind Fortune
           and have mercy on a daughter undone by love.
           My own mother erred out of love,
           and you know what that cost me.
           Take heed from this example and so many others.
           We know that Fortune's lightning
           always strikes the tallest towers.

ENGLAND   (*To* PRIMISLAO) You are now undeceived,
           and know the prince of Scotland is innocent.   3020

PRIMISLAO I'm already shedding tender tears
           for my dear, dead Teodosia.

ENGLAND   Then lock up Faustina, that beast.
           And so you will have sons to succeed you in this kingdom,
           the prince of Scotland offers you his sister in marriage.

TEODOSIA   Grant me license to speak, my lords,
           though I am but a humble farmer.
           If King Primislao hopes for a successor,
           he need not remarry.
           His heir is right here.   3030

PRIMISLAO Here? What are you saying?

TEODOSIA   Here, my lord.

PRIMISLAO Who?

TEODOSIA   That wild thing called the "Beast of Hungary"
            whom you have here in chains.
            She is that babe Faustina gave birth to
            in the woods on that fateful day.

PRIMISLAO   That is quite a tall tale
            you've made up for your own gain.

FELIPE   Listen to him, my lord.   3040
            He surely speaks the truth.
            I have loved her since I first saw her in the woods.
            She has rare intellect and matchless beauty.
            She even looks like you!

ENGLAND   Though what he says may be true,
            you cannot hand your kingdom to a beast
            without greater proof.
            You should have this villain tortured!

TEODOSIA   (*Aside*) So much sorrow over so many years!

PRIMISLAO   Well said.   3050
            Call in the torturers!

TEODOSIA   If I could produce a witness to my story,
            would you believe it then?

ENGLAND   There is none who could convince me.
            No sane person would believe it.

PRIMISLAO   Even if I were to see my dead queen,
            Teodosia, suddenly come back to life,
            even if she were to tell me this is my daughter,
            I still would not believe it.

TEODOSIA   My lord, I am Teodosia.   3060

PRIMISLAO	What?
ENGLAND	How?
TEODOSIA	I am the queen. I lived in those mountains in the form and fashion of a beast, and I took the child.
PRIMISLAO	Teodosia, let me see your face. It's you, no doubt.
ENGLAND	My daughter!
PRIMISLAO	My wife! 3070
TEODOSIA	Do not believe for a second that you can return to my arms without first promising me two things: that Felipe will marry Rosaura and take her to Spain; and that Faustina will be pardoned, as long as she takes religious vows.
PRIMISLAO	I agree. I give my daughter to Felipe.

FELIPE unties ROSAURA

FELIPE	My beloved beast, I will take you from these chains and into my arms.
ENGLAND	And I pardon Faustina. 3080
FELIPE	The author now begs this audience to forgive his errors,

as he labors only to serve you.[38]
From beginning to end,
you have heard the true story
of that great Beast of Hungary,
of whom the chronicles tell.

---

38   *Comedias* often end in a brief address to the audience.

www.ingramcontent.com/pod-product-compliance
Lightning Source LLC
Chambersburg PA
CBHW022105160426
43198CB00008B/361